UNDENIABLE
EVIDENCE

RAY COMFORT

BRIDGE
LOGOS

Newberry, FL 32669

Bridge-Logos
Newberry, FL 32669

Undeniable Evidence:
Ten of the Top Scientific Facts in the Bible
by Ray Comfort

Printed in the United States of America

Library of Congress Catalog Card Number: 2019931777

International Standard Book Number: 978-1-61036-408-9

Edited by Lynn Copeland

Cover design by Genesis Group (genesis-group.net)

Interior design by Kent Jensen (knail.com) with special thanks to Lynn Copeland
for artistic direction.

VP 01 05/2019

CONTENTS

INTRODUCTION

IF THE BIBLE IS TRUE

If the Bible is truly the Word of God, the implications are unspeakably wonderful, and at the same time utterly terrifying. This is because of its offer of Heaven and its warning of Hell. As believers, we know that the Bible is God's Word, but how effectively can we convince others of that truth?

In this book we will look at the case for the Scriptures being divinely inspired, by looking at empirical evidence to back up the claim—what could be considered to be ten of the top scientific facts in the Bible.

The challenge to those the Bible calls the "unsaved" is that they owe it to themselves (and those they love) to examine the facts to see if the Bible is truly God's message to humanity. Is the gospel Heaven-sent? In an unstable world that is growing darker by the day, here is something to rest our hopes on and relieve our fears—both for this life and for the life to come. The word *gospel* means "good news," but it's only good news if we see ourselves as we really are in the sight of God.

Years ago, Mark Spence, who works for our ministry, taught a weekly Bible study with about twenty women attending. It was wonderful that they had such a hunger for the Word of God. At one of the studies Mark announced some really good news. He had become engaged. The next week no one showed up at his study. It was understandable that they weren't too happy, because Mark was tall, dark, and handy around the house with tools. What may be good news to some people may not be good news to others.

So it is with the gospel. It is God's offer of everlasting life to dying humanity, but most don't see that as being good news at all. Not even slightly. Not even if we have solid evidence to back up its claim. If you're a true-blue skeptic, you can easily negate the evidence simply by not accepting it. You could say that these "solid facts" were added to the Bible after the fact, or that the author never intended for his words to be interpreted in such a way. Or you may say that establishing the existence of God doesn't prove that this God is the Christian one. That leaves the claims of the gospel going nowhere.

The eloquent and likable atheist Christopher Hitchens, now deceased, once said,

> But if you've established deism you've got all your work still ahead of you to be a theist. You have to show that this god, this person who went to all this trouble with physics, cares

who you sleep with or how or whether you should eat pig or not or what day you should observe as holy.[1]

Good point. How do we move from believing that Something created everything to the thought that this Something cares about you committing adultery? The answer isn't difficult, as we will look at later in this book. As Christians, we often point to prophecy as evidence that the message of the Bible is divine. The Scriptures predict the future in many places, and because mankind can't even predict tomorrow's weather accurately, we maintain that the words of the Bible must be written by the hand of God.

As a hard-nosed skeptic, you could maintain that if we fire 100 arrows into the air, one of them will eventually hit some target, and that that's what happens with prophecy. If there are enough predictions, one or two are bound to get it right That's true in one sense. Think of the famed prophecies of Nostradamus. His ramblings were so nebulous about supposed events that would take place, you can look at almost anything in history and find a convincing target, and it will sound credible to the simple.

This is especially the case with those who don't know their Bibles. Nostradamus secretly read the Scriptures, stole some of its prophetic words and made them his own, giving him credibility with those who are ignorant of what Scripture says. And so his prophecies have become big business for publishers and filmmakers who have a huge financial incentive to convince the world to believe them.

However, there is much more at stake than money when it comes to an unbelieving world accepting the message of the

Bible. It is no big deal whether you believe Nostradamus; there are no consequences for not believing his prophecies. But there are dire consequences for not believing what the Bible says. This is because genuine belief always produces some sort of reaction. A hand grenade tossed at your feet will cause you to run, if you *believe* that the pin has been pulled and you're in danger. If you don't believe, you will probably just stand where you are. If you and I truly believe what the Bible says about Heaven and Hell, we will react accordingly. For those who think belief is for weak people, one ticking time-bomb tossed at the their feet will show their thoughtlessness in seconds.

YOUR MIDLIFE CRISIS

Millions have what is erroneously called a "mid-life crisis." It is incorrectly labeled, because nobody knows the time of the middle of their life. The only way to pinpoint that would be to know the date of your death. If you know that you will die at age eighty-six, when you turn forty-three you can then say that you are having a midlife crisis, if indeed you are distressed about life.

What most are having would be better termed a *realization of their mortality*. They come to the realization that they are dying, and the crisis is that they believe there's nothing they can do about it. There is an ever-darkening shadow over them as the Grim Reaper inevitably closes in.

But because Christians *have* done something about it, they don't have any crisis. Believers don't resign themselves *to* the inevitability of death, they resign *from* it. We overcome death in Christ. Until this good news is realized and embraced, the world will have an ever-increasing and terrifying crisis until death seizes upon them. That's why we must plead with the lost as if tonight their soul is going to be required of them.

If you're not a believer, it may surprise you to know that my agenda isn't to convince you that the Bible is God-inspired. It's rather to convince you to believe one relatively small part of the Bible—the gospel. That "good news."

The gospel is the simple but profound message that Jesus Christ suffered and died for our sins and rose again on the third day. The Scriptures make it even more simple by saying that Jesus "has abolished death and brought life and immortality to light through the gospel" (2 Timothy 1:10).

To any thinking unbeliever, that statement by itself is ridiculous. People die at the rate of 150,000 every 24 hours. It is senseless, naïve, and annoyingly stupid to think that Jesus has abolished death. That is, until we understand the *nature* of death. Scripture tells us that it's a wage (see Romans 6:23). Death here on earth is the first payout. We *earn* capital punishment for our sins. That's a bitter pill to swallow for a world that embraces humanism—a philosophical worldview that paints mankind as being unworthy of such terrible condemnation. Hard to believe though it may be, death is the ultimate convincing agent that God is deadly serious about sin. Actually it's more than just a convincing agent. It is the arresting officer that will drag us before the Judge of the Universe to stand trial for violating His moral Law, and those who are found guilty will find themselves in God's prison . . . a terrible place called Hell, and there's no parole.

Yet, there is something that precedes the gospel and helps it make sense, and it's something far more convincing than scientific or prophetic facts. This is why I have included a number of true-life gospel presentations in this book. To illustrate the importance of this, let me ask you an easy question. When a blind man boarded a crowded bus, someone immediately stood and gave up his seat. Here's the question: Was that a good thing to do? The answer seems obvious. Of course it was! It was kind and thoughtful. Yet it wasn't; it was morally wrong and foolish. It was so wrong, when his boss heard that he had given up his seat, he was fired. And rightly so. This is because he was the *driver*.

Knowing that he was the driver quickly changes our perspective. This is because we were given information that reshaped our thinking.

That's the reason I have also included the "something" that precedes the gospel presentation. It contains vital information that, if believed, will radically change our minds about the gospel. Instead of it being irrelevant and naïve foolishness, it becomes the greatest news you could ever hope to hear.

And even though I've included these, my confidence isn't confined to the information you will read. It is in the God who gave us the gospel. In John 16:8, when Jesus spoke of the ministry of the Holy Spirit, He said,

> "And when He has come, He will convict the world of sin,
> and of righteousness, and of judgment..."

The intent of a good prosecutor is to convict a guilty criminal. When a sinner is convicted of his sins, understands that he has failed to reach the moral standard expected of him, and is therefore under judgment for his crimes, he's ready for the good news of the gospel. The conviction of the Holy Spirit convinces us that we are sinners. That was my experience, and the experience of millions, and is what brings us to the cross. This is because sin, righteousness, and judgment are *moral* issues rather than intellectual ones. The Holy Spirit didn't come to *intellectually* convince us that the Bible is God's Word. That should be the *result* of conversion, not the *means*. No one comes to the Savior without a knowledge of sin. If we don't think we need to be saved from our sins, we don't think we need the Savior.

The scientific facts in this book serve as a light for the intellect, but as mentioned, this light can easily be extinguished. However, the real-life witnessing sessions at the end of each chapter contain light for the conscience. And *that* light isn't so easy to extinguish. Though the conscience may be society-shaped, it is independent and God-given. It can be dulled, but it has a way of flickering back to life and shining so brightly that it has driven many to drink, and some to suicide.

My hope is that the light it brings drives you to the Savior, and in doing so shows you that Jesus Christ has abolished death and brought life and immortality to light through the gospel. That's good news for those who value their life. *Really* good news.

ANOTHER REASON

There is another important reason that I've included the real-life gospel conversations throughout this publication. The purpose of the Church on earth is to fulfill the Great Commission (see Matthew 28:18–20). Jesus suffered and died so that sinners could be saved from death and Hell—that's the message we are to take to this dying world. However, according to a recent Barna Group survey, 51 percent of the contemporary Church have never even *heard* of the Great Commission, another 6 percent weren't sure what it was, and 25 percent said they couldn't recall exactly what it was meant.[2] That left only 17 percent of the Church knowing what the Great Commission meant—even fewer actually obeying the command to go into all the world and make disciples, and even fewer knowing how to do this biblically.

In his book *The Coming Revival*, Bill Bright reported that "only two percent of believers in America regularly share their faith in Christ with others."[3] My hope is that you will find the witnessing encounters inspiring and encouraging and that you will then want to share your faith with others. But, if you are normal, you may have a small problem.

YOUR LINGUAL FRENULUM

Do you know what it means to be "tongue tied"? It's when someone is unable to speak because of shyness or embarrassment. If you are shy or embarrassed when it comes to sharing your faith, let me share a fascinating story that points to a solution.

In April 2017, a six-year-old boy from Texas visited a pediatric dentist for work on his teeth. For most of his life he was unable to speak clearly. His speech was so unintelligible that the only ones who could understand what he was saying were his parents.

During the dental procedure the dentist noticed that the boy was tongue-tied, a condition in which his lingual frenulum—the band of tissue under his tongue—was shorter than normal, keeping him from moving it freely. She ran to the waiting room to ask his parents if she could snip it. They gave permission, and after a ten-second procedure, the boy immediately spoke clearly.

We see a similar incident in Mark 7:32–35 when Jesus prayed for a man whom the Bible says "was deaf and had an impediment in his speech." Jesus said, "Be opened," and the Scriptures say, "Immediately his ears were opened, and the impediment of his tongue was loosed, and he spoke plainly." His ears were opened, then he spoke clearly.

If you're tongue-tied when it comes to the gospel, let me perform a quick and simple operation that will almost certainly fix the problem. The problem is that your conscience is falling short of what it should be doing. This may be a little painful, but what I'm going to say should free it up, so that it does its God-given duty. If your ears are open to what I'm about to say, you will begin to speak clearly, and if that happens it will change your life forever.

Here goes:

Charles Spurgeon said, "Have you no wish for others to be saved? Then you are not saved yourself. Be sure of that." You're more concerned with your own temporary embarrassment than you are with the fact that people are going to Hell for eternity. How then can you say that the love of God dwells within you? If you're not deeply concerned for the salvation of the lost, I'm deeply concerned for yours.

There you are. I hope that helps. You should be able to speak clearly—if you have a mind to do so. And as you begin to move in that direction, those witnessing encounters will help you to have confidence.

Now that we understand why witnessing conversations are included in this book, let's look at a few scientific facts in the Bible. In chapters 1 through 10, we'll consider ten of the top scientific facts recorded in Scripture. To help you recall the points that are covered, each of these chapters includes "Questions to Consider" for you to ponder (or to discuss if you're reading in a group) before going on to the next chapter.

THE EARTH'S FREE-FLOAT IN SPACE

Do you ever think about the fact that we are living on a massive round rock that is suspended in space? Of course, that is being a little simplistic. While we *are* hanging in space, we are spinning in a circle and moving through this vast universe. With the advent of space travel, we have even more answers, but the answers only bring up more questions. How does our planet spin, why does it spin, what made it spin, how does it move through space, when did all this begin, what caused the earth to hang in space, what is space, and where did *that* come from?

Secular science prides itself on its answer-seeking as to *how, what, when, where,* and *why.* But it stops for some reason at *who.* But why omit *who*? If truth is our goal, we must follow wherever it goes, even if it leads to an uncomfortable *Who.*

THE VERY LARGE ANIMAL

At a time in history when it was believed by some that the earth sat on a large animal (around 1500 BC), the Bible spoke of the earth's free float in space:

He stretches out the north over empty space; He hangs the earth on nothing. (Job 26:7)

There we see the *Who* in the double mention of the word "He." According to the Bible, the earth's spin, its movement through space, and its free float weren't an accident. It was purposefully *placed* by God.

I'm going to repeat myself a number of times in this publication, by being aghast to a point of mind-blown numbness at the power of God. How on earth could He have created this earth, suspended it in the almost nothingness of space, spinning it like a top, from the top to the bottom? How could He have then flicked it like a massive marble and set it in motion through space, in a circuit? But that's what happened: "In the beginning God created the heavens and the earth" (Genesis 1:1). Sometimes we are so focused on the *when* of the "beginning" that we overlook the *how* or the *Who*. He hung the earth on nothing! Our normally most applicable "WOW!" falls woefully short.

Science didn't discover that the earth hangs on nothing until 1650 AD, 3,000 years later:

Discovered in 1475 by Copernicus, astronomers found that the earth hangs literally on nothing, or is free floating in space. Other cultures from around the world at this time, when examined show the way that human cultures thought about astronomy and how the nature of the earth worked by man's understanding. Hindus believed that the earth was held on the back of four elephants standing on the back of a cosmic turtle, Akupara. In Greek mythology, it was believed that the god Atlas held the earth upon his back, written by the poet Hesiod. The Norse mythology exclaims the earth, along with 8 other worlds, are held up by a giant ash tree, Yggdrasil.[4]

In the 1680s, Sir Isaac Newton discovered that the earth was suspended in outer space, being held in orbit by the gravitational force of the sun. It was not until recent times that man has proved Newton's theory by way of space flights.[5]

THE UNBELIEVER

The simplicity of "He hangs the earth on nothing" isn't so readily embraced by the understandable bias of a hard-nosed skeptic. He doesn't want this to be evidence of divine inspiration, because it is the ultimate of wet blankets on his deliriously pleasurable sins. So he will search his fertile imagination (and the Scriptures) for evidence to the contrary, and there he will find enough rope to hang himself. Here is one skeptic imagining Job's thoughts:

Firstly, the odds of just *guessing* this fact correctly are pretty good, since either the earth hangs on something, or it does not. You have one chance in two of guessing correctly. And the odds are even better when we consider that Job could observe that:

1) There was nothing visibly tethering the earth to the sky,

2) The sun and moon did not hang on anything, and

3) The sun appeared to go down in the West and rise in the East, and nothing impeded its path (suggesting there was nothing underneath the earth, just as there was nothing under the sun or the moon).

Given this, such a revelation isn't impossible or even unreasonable.[6]

It may be reasonable for an atheist—someone who believes the scientific impossibility that nothing created everything. Such a revelation also isn't impossible for someone so gullible as to believe that mankind evolved from primates when there isn't a lone bone to back up the belief. Neither can it pass the scientific method of being tested or observed.

But it is utterly unreasonable for any rational human being who sees the effects of gravity on a leaf, or even a tiny feather, to believe for a second that a lowly rock—let alone this massive earth—could hang lighter than a feather on nothing. Such a belief would be ridiculous, in the truest sense of the word.

The skeptic then turns to the pages of Scripture:

Secondly, if it turned out the earth *wasn't* floating, but was supported in some way, there are numerous verses that could've been used to suggest God always knew that the earth was supported:

"He shakes the earth from its place and makes its pillars tremble." —Job 9:6

"Where wast thou when I laid the foundations of the earth?...Whereupon are the foundations thereof fastened?" —Job 38:4–6

"The pillars of the earth are the LORD's, and he hath set the world upon them." —1 Samuel 2:8

"When the earth and all its people quake, it is I who hold its pillars firm." —Psalm 75:3

Since there are only two possibilities (floating or supported), and both are suggested in the Bible, the Bible has a 100% chance of getting this fact correct (so long as we play down the losing answer).

With the benefit of hindsight (and a little bias), today's believer can now assert that *all* the verses about pillars *must* be metaphorical, while the single verse about hanging on nothing *must* be interpreted literally.[7]

Typically, the skeptic thinks that his thoughts are exhaustive. He offers only two explanations:

1. Physical pillars, or,
2. The free float in space.

But there is at least one other explanation, given over three hundred years ago. John Gill's commentary (originally published in 1766) gives a third explanation, and clearly the correct one for the use of the word *pillars*:

The earth has its foundations on which it is laid, and its pillars by which it is supported; but these are no other than the power and providence of God; otherwise the earth is hung upon nothing, in the open circumambient air: and that God can and does do this may well be thought, and to do all the above things in providence and grace, related in the preceding verses; in the support, and for the proof of which, this is observed. Figuratively, the pillars of the earth may design the princes of the world, the supreme rulers of it, and civil magistrates, who are sometimes called corner-stones, and the shields of the earth (Zechariah 10:4; Psalm 47:9), and so pillars, because they are the means of cementing, supporting, and protecting the people of the earth, and of preserving their peace and property. Likewise good men may be meant in a figurative sense, who, as they are the salt of the earth, are the pillars of it, for whose sake it was made, and is supported, and continued in being; the church is the pillar and ground of truth; and every good man is a pillar in the house of God, and especially ministers of the Gospel.[8]

Here are the verses that refer to men as metaphoric pillars:

"He who overcomes, I will make him a pillar in the temple of My God, and he shall go out no more. I will write on him the name of My God and the name of the city of My God, the New Jerusalem, which comes down out of heaven from My God. And I will write on him My new name." (Revelation 3:12)

"But if I am delayed, I write so that you may know how you ought to conduct yourself in the house of God, which is the church of the living God, the pillar and ground of the truth." (1 Timothy 3:15)

"And when James, Cephas, and John, who seemed to be pillars, perceived the grace that had been given to me, they gave me and Barnabas the right hand of fellowship, that we should go to the Gentiles and they to the circumcised." (Galatians 2:9)

"Wisdom has built her house, she has hewn out her seven pillars" (Proverbs 9:1)

WAIT A MINUTE

Weight Watchers and a thousand other weighty organizations want us to watch our weight. In one sense, they exist because they work alongside the junk food and fast food folks. They feed off each other. We pay one to put it on, and we pay the other to take it off. Our intake is their income. Bible verses such as "And put a knife to your throat if you are a man given to appetite" (Proverbs 23:2), if obeyed, would put both out of business.

The dictionary tells us that *weight* is "a body's relative mass or the quantity of matter contained by it, giving rise to a downward force; the heaviness of a person or thing." But our *real* concern, more than our weight, is our quantity of fat. If we looked lean and were rippled with muscle, it probably wouldn't worry us too much how much we weighed, because we would look good.

Have you ever thought about how much this earth weighs? Think of the weight of all the oceans, the massive mountains around the earth, the elephants, the whales, and all the other animals, plus almost seven billion people, many of whom are overweight. It's pretty heavy:

> So what does Earth weigh? Earth's weight is 5.972 sextillion (1,000 trillion) metric tons... That's 5,972,000,000,-000,000,000,000 tons and gaining.[9]

Such measurements are beyond our comprehension. But what we *can* know is that the Bible says God created every atom that holds every drop of water in the massive oceans, the magnificent mountains, shaped it all into one big ball, and hung it on nothing in space. These are heavy thoughts.

EARTH'S MAKEUP

Do you ever think about what makes up the earth? Its outer crust is made of what we often call *soil*, or the dust of the earth. Many unbelievers believe we came from dust—star dust—because our bodies are made up of the same elements that are in the soil. According to Physics.org, "We are all made of stardust."[10]

> For decades, science popularizers have said humans are made of stardust, and now, a new survey of 150,000 stars shows just how true the old cliché is: Humans and their galaxy have about 97 percent of the same kind of atoms, and the elements of life appear to be more prevalent toward the galaxy's center, the research found. The crucial elements for

life on Earth, often called the building blocks of life, can be abbreviated as CHNOPS: carbon, hydrogen, nitrogen, oxygen, phosphorus and sulfur. For the first time, astronomers have cataloged the abundance of these elements in a huge sample of stars.[11]

But we already knew that we are from dust, because thousands of years ago the book of Genesis says that God made man from the dust of the earth:

And the LORD God formed man of the dust of the ground, and breathed into his nostrils the breath of life; and man became a living being. (Genesis 2:7)

And we're not the only life that comes from the soil. All of our food comes from the soil. All plants, fruit trees, etc., obtain their life from the earth as they grow in its crust, and all animals eat food that traces itself back to the soil. We trample dirt beneath our feet, but without it, we wouldn't be alive.

And so this great big, incredibly heavy ball of dirt floats in space, seemingly lighter than a feather, because God put it there. Do you believe that? If you don't, would you let the evidence take you there?

Richard Dawkins became the most famous atheist of our time, but before he evolved into that role, there was another atheist who was held in high esteem by the world. His name was Antony Flew, an English philosopher who taught at universities such as Oxford. According to Wikipedia:

Belonging to the analytic and evidentialist schools of thought, Flew was most notable for his work related to the philosophy of religion...For much of his career Flew was known as a strong advocate of atheism, arguing that one should presuppose atheism until empirical evidence of a God surfaces. He also criticized the idea of life after death, the free will defense to the problem of evil, and the meaningfulness of the concept of God.

However, in 2004 he changed his position, to acknowledge the existence of an Intelligent Creator of the universe, shocking his fellow colleagues and atheists...He stated that in keeping his lifelong commitment to go where the evidence leads, he now believed in the existence of a God.[12]

It was the discovery of DNA that stopped Flew in his atheist tracks. Asked if recent work on the origin of life pointed to a creative Intelligence, this is what he said:

Yes, I now think it does...almost entirely because of the DNA investigations. What I think the DNA material has done is that it has shown, by the almost unbelievable complexity of the arrangements which are needed to produce (life), that intelligence must have been involved in getting these extraordinarily diverse elements to work together.[13]

In his book *There Is a God*, Flew later explained how he arrived at his conclusion:

Science spotlights three dimensions of nature that point to God. The first is the fact that nature obeys laws. The second is the dimension of life, of intelligently organized and purpose-driven beings, which arose from matter. The third is the very existence of nature. But it is not science alone that has guided me. I have also been helped by a renewed study of the classical philosophical arguments.[14]

One would think that his much publicized conversion to theism would have led others to rethink their views and brought an end to the foolishness of atheism. But it didn't. This is because most who profess atheism are not like Flew. They stumble at *Who.* There is good reason for that.

PAPER MONEY

Did you know that American currency is made of cotton? It feels like paper, but it's not:

According to the Bureau of Engraving and Printing, US paper currency is made up of 75% cotton and 25% linen. That is, there are three-fourths of a pound of cotton in each pound of dollar bills. This same source also informs us that there are 454 bills in a pound of currency. During Fiscal Year 2009, over six billion bills of all denominations were printed in the United States, consuming 21,476 bales of cotton. The total dollar value of these bills was two hundred and nineteen billion dollars, or $21,290.55 per pound of cotton.[15]

Let's surmise that a skeptic doesn't believe money is made of cotton, so he says the cotton folks are all lying for some reason. He then points to a government organization to back up his claim.

It's an article from the US Treasury's Bureau of Engraving and Printing that is headlined "How Money is Made—Paper and Ink":

> The paper and ink used in the production of U.S. paper currency is as distinct as its design. The paper, with the exception of $100 paper, comes to the BEP in brown paper-wrapped loads of 20,000 sheets (two pallets of 10,000 sheets). $100 paper comes to the BEP in loads of 16,000 sheets (two pallets of 8,000). Each of these sheets is tracked and accounted for as it passes through the production process.[16]

He then has you count how many times the word "paper" is used, saying, "Paper money is made of paper, not cotton." You check out the article, but further down you read:

> The ordinary paper that consumers use throughout their everyday life such as newspapers, books, cereal boxes, etc., is primarily made of wood pulp; however, United States currency paper is composed of 75 percent cotton and 25 percent linen.[17]

But he replies that he doesn't believe what the government says because it's in cahoots with the cotton industry. You therefore point to an independent news source:

> NEW YORK (CNNMoney)—Sure, packs of T-shirts and socks are getting expensive because of skyrocketing cotton prices. Guess what else is made of cotton? The dollar bill in your wallet.

In 2010, the cost of making one note jumped 50% from what it cost the government in 2008.

The government produced 6.4 billion new currency notes last year. Each one cost 9.6 cents to produce, including the cost of paper and printing.

In 2008, it only cost 6.4 cents a note, a tiny bit more than it did in 2007, according to the U.S. Bureau of Engraving and Printing.

With the price of raw cotton at a 140-year high, things could get worse.[18]

He says that it's fake news. So you have a dilemma. All the evidence you present to him is cut off at the pass. Nothing can or will convince him if he refuses to have some sort of faith. If he doesn't believe what's presented, there is no case for him to be considering.

There is also another problem: he may be right. The government *could* be lying—a lie that has been believed by the media and others. It may come out in years later that billions of dollars has been pocketed over the years by corrupt government officials, who perpetuated the lie that money is made of expensive cotton, when it was really made with a cheap but strong papyrus reed.

So when it comes down to the truth, we don't truly know if American paper money *really* is made of cotton. Even if we have it professionally analyzed, we have to have faith in those results. We can only believe it, and that belief may change with further knowledge.

Everything we think is true falls into the same category. Many things that were believed two hundred years ago have been proven to be false, and our present scientifically believed conclusions may be laughed at as being ludicrous two centuries from now. And yet truth itself doesn't change. Whatever makes up paper money remains the same, despite our surmising.

Antony Flew, who believed he had discovered the truth, stated:

> I have been denounced by my fellow unbelievers for stupidity, betrayal, senility and everything you could think of. And none of them have read a word that I have ever written.[19]

Unlike Flew, most atheists aren't interested in following where the truth leads. No matter what we tell them about the existence of God, they have the option of choice. They can always come back with an argument. That our creation had a Creator is as obvious as a building is proof of the builder and a painting is proof of the painter. But if the skeptic has a mind to, he can play semantics. He can cut everything off through unbelief. He can say that he doesn't believe the building is proof of a builder, nor a painting is evidence of the painter—and so, for us, Reason Street becomes a dead end.

If someone has ever listened to the song of a bird, felt the warmth of the sun, viewed the blueness of the sky, smelled the fragrance of a rose, held a puppy in his arms, looked into the eyes of a newborn baby, and said to himself that it all happened accidentally because of an explosion of nothing in space—caused by nothing—then I must concede that the Bible is right when it says that person is a fool (see Psalm 14:1). Atheism is a form of willful insanity.

FISHING WITH MY DOG

For years I have wanted to buy the world's biggest breed of dog. I'm talking about a Great Dane *plus*. This was because I caught a glimpse of their potential to reach the lost. I had noticed that when someone had a huge dog, strangers would approach the owner and start a conversation. If I had a massive canine it would simply be a matter of getting to know the person who approached me, and then transitioning to the gospel.

I had already created a gospel tract that included trivia on dogs and tips on how to easily train them. But I hesitated to buy a huge dog for a number of reasons: 1) He may eat my existing smallish dog, Sam. 2) Our backyard is the size of a postage stamp, so he would have trouble turning around. 3) It would cost an arm and a big leg to feed. 4) There are big daily repercussions when you give a big dog big food. 5) Vet bills would be off the charts.

But one Saturday as Sam ran alongside my bike, I noticed that he couldn't run the distance he did as a puppy. I scooped him up and carried him with one arm, but he was so heavy that by the time we got home, my arm was screaming with pain. So I decided to make a contraption for him to sit on in front of me—between my arms as I rode the bike.

The platform I made wasn't too stable, so I decided to call a local garage to ask if they did welding. The owner looked at what I had made and gave me some great advice to make it stable. His name was Nasser. He was a Muslim, but he let me briefly share the gospel with him. Then he said the whole thing was pretty confusing because he was listening to the radio and heard a Catholic priest say that he was into Buddhism.

The first time I went for a ride with Sam, I stopped in to see Nasser, thanked him for his advice, and gave him one of my books. He seemed really pleased.

The next day I went for a ride on the bike, but this time I put a pair of sunglasses on Sam that matched the pair I was wearing. Suddenly, strangers began pointing and smiling, and yelling out, "Cute dog!!" When I stopped for a pat and chat, it was like we were old friends. I realized that I didn't need a big dog. *Cute* had the same effect.

FIRST WITNESSING SESSION

When I saw three men in their early twenties sitting on a park bench smoking marijuana, I rode right up to them and begin talking. It wasn't even slightly awkward. This was because they were smiling at my dog wearing sunglasses. Sam was a wonderfully effective icebreaker. They even offered me a puff of marijuana. I said that I didn't need it, and had a great time witnessing to them for about fifteen minutes.

Some time later, Sam paved the way for me to approach a young man who was sitting in a local park reading a book. His name was Alex, and he was an atheist who was honest enough to admit that if he faced the Ten Commandments on Judgment Day he would be justly damned in Hell. (We'll see later why I asked him this.)

Then I asked a probing question I always ask the lost. I said, "Does that concern you?" A second later we talked over each other. Just as he replied, "No," I said, "Think before you answer, because I'm going to question you about your answer." He did think, and immediately changed his mind to, "Yes, it does, actually." The thought of going to Hell terrified him. But this was a good fear because it was a fear of *real* danger.

The prospect of dropping 10,000 feet from a plane is a good fear that sends us running to a parachute, and the prospect of passing through death without the Savior is terrifying for those who think. Those who don't think will stay in their sins and have eternity to regret not manning-up to their sins and its fearful consequences.

In the movie *After Earth*, actor Will Smith's character said, "Fear is not real. The only place that fear can exist is in our thoughts of the future. It is a product of our imagination, causing us to fear things that do not at present and may not ever exist. Do not misunderstand me, danger is very real, but fear is a choice."

In one sense that is correct. But if we don't have faith in God, we have nothing with which to replace fear. The psalmist said, "The LORD is on my side; I will not fear. What can man do to me?" (Psalm 118:6). "I will not fear" is a choice. The psalmist chooses not to fear, but he has that choice only because of his faith in God.

Having no fear may be valid when talking about achieving goals in life, or working the stock market, or having faith in yourself when making decisions. But for the unsaved there is an inner fear over which they have no control without faith in God—namely, the fear of death. Death is the future's promise, whether we are rich or poor, famous or unknown, wise or a fool.

It is the great leveler and a Goliath that feeds its victims to the birds. Reject God, and that fear produces unending torment.

Making sinners tremble in fear at the thought of facing God is something believers should never fear. It is the greatest favor we could ever do for those the Bible calls "lost." The result of Paul's faithful preaching to Felix the governor was that "Felix was afraid" (Acts 24:25), and that fear came because the apostle spoke the truth in love. If we love the unsaved, then we must tell them that it is a "fearful thing to fall into the hands of the living God" (Hebrews 10:31).

That's what I did with this humble atheist, and the result of his humility was that he let me pray with him. If we want to see sinners come to the cross we must not be afraid to make them afraid, and the way we deal with a fear of doing so is to have faith in God. He is our helper as we share the gospel, and it's ultimately His smile we seek.

MY WIFE IS MISSING

There is an interesting story about a man whose wife disappeared:

Husband: My wife is missing. She went shopping yesterday and hasn't come home!

Officer: Age?

Husband: I'm not sure. Somewhere between 50 and 60. We don't do birthdays.

Officer: Height?

Husband: I'm not sure. A little over five feet tall.

Officer: Weight?

Husband: Don't know. Not slim, not really heavy.

Officer: Color of eyes?

Husband: Sort of brown, I think. Never really noticed.

Officer: Color of hair?

Husband: Changes a couple times a year. Maybe dark brown now. I can't remember.

Officer: What was she wearing?

Husband: Could have been pants, or maybe a skirt or shorts. I don't know exactly.

Officer: What kind of car was she in?

Husband: She went in my truck.

Officer: What kind of truck was it?

Husband: A 2017, manufactured September 16th, pearl white Ram Limited 4X4 with 6.4l Hemi V8 engine ordered with the Ram Box bar and fridge option, LED lighting, backup and front camera, moose-hide leather heated and cooled seats, climate-controlled air-conditioning. It has a custom matching white cover for the bed, Weather Tech floor mats, trailing package with gold hitch, sunroof, DVD, with full GPS navigation, satellite radio, Cobra 75 WX ST 40-channel CB radio, six cup holders, 3 USB ports, and 4 power outlets. I added special alloy wheels and off-road Toyo tires. It has custom retracting running boards and under-glow wheel well lighting.

(At this point the husband started choking up.)

Officer: Take it easy, sir. We'll find your truck.

Of course, that was just a joke. But it *does* make a valid point. We focus on things that we care about. This is the motivation for us to study on how to reach the lost. Love cares.

ANOTHER ENCOUNTER

Sam and I were out on the bike. I had prayed for divine encounters yet had spoken to only one person, and he didn't want to talk. He was very polite, but he was working out on the basketball court, so I didn't pressure him.

About a minute later I saw a gentleman walking toward me, and I gave him a coin containing the Ten Commandments and the gospel.[20] When his reaction was positive, I asked him if he was a Christian. Sye said he was, "...sort of." I questioned as to what he meant, and he responded that things weren't going too well. I asked him, "Isn't that the time that we should be driven to our knees?" He agreed.

When I asked him if he was a good person he said that he was, and so we went through the Ten Commandments, into the cross and his need to repent and trust Jesus. He is very thankful for some literature and a Subway gift card I gave him. Just as I was about to say goodbye, another gentleman walked up and asked if he could take a photograph of Sam wearing sunglasses.

I said goodbye to Sye and went through exactly the same approach with this next gentleman, whose name was Dustin. Dustin was in his mid-twenties, wearing cool sunglasses, but his face was terribly disfigured by some sort of physical virus. It looked as though the virus had exploded and almost blocked out one side of his face. My heart went out to him. If I get as much as a pimple on my nose I'm horrified. Despite this man's scars, he was as happy as a lark. His positive demeanor gave me a sense of admiration for him.

Dustin said that he was a good person and as we went through the Commandments, he held on to his self-righteousness. So I explained that the confusion comes with the definition of the word "good." It means moral perfection—in thought, word, and deed. When I shared the gospel with him, he was very appreciative and thankful.

It always amazes me that, even though I had gone through the same thing word-for-word with two different gentleman within just ten minutes, I didn't tire for a second when sharing such an incredibly wonderful message. It was as though it was my first time.

A few days later, I saw a young man sitting in a grassy area at a park. I rode up to him, gave him a Ten Commandments coin, and asked if he ever thought about the afterlife. He did but not much. I said it was probably because he was young. He nodded in agreement.

When I asked him if he was going to Heaven when he died— was he a good person?—he was a little uncomfortable, but politely let me speak. After taking him through the gospel, I thanked him for listening to me, and when I gave him a Subway gift card he said, "Wow!" His attitude completely changed, and he became thankful that I'd talked to him about his eternal salvation.

A minute or so later as I was riding the bike, a woman stopped me. She raved about Sam and the fact that he was wearing sunglasses. She said that she was a Christian, but I detected that something wasn't right. So I gave her a CD and encouraged her to watch our Living Waters YouTube videos.

A few feet in front of us, an elderly gentleman had a metal detector and was digging into the park grass, searching for coins. So I gave him a Ten Commandments coin. He said that he was a Christian, but that he wasn't born again. I told him that the difference between being born again and believing in God is like the difference between wearing a parachute and just believing in one when 10,000 feet up in a plane. I said that when we jump we will see the difference. Then I told him it was essential that he was born again. He seemed a little agitated, so I asked if he was comfortable talking about spiritual things. He said he was, but a little later said that he didn't discuss religion and politics. I laughed and said, "I bet you talk about politics but you just want me to leave," so I gave him a Subway gift card, and as I did, I was able to share the gospel with him in a 30-second presentation. Then I smiled and said, "Well, I got it in." Thankfully, he smiled back.

QUESTIONS TO CONSIDER

1. How does mentioning the earth's free float in space give the Bible credibility?
2. Explain how the earth could hang on nothing.
3. Try to justify the logic of believing that the earth sits on something.
4. Are you brought to wordless worship at the thought of the power of God? If so, why?

⑤ How should we live our lives when we understand the power of God?

⑥ Name a good fear to have. Why is it good?

⑦ Read Acts 24:24,25 and explain what it was that made Felix afraid.

2

STARS ARE INNUMERABLE

One of the greatest honors for this world is to be given a star on the Hollywood Walk of Fame. If you have celebrity, people from all over the world honor you by stopping and excitedly taking pictures of your name "immortalized" in the sidewalk. They feel a unique sense of connection. If you're not known, they walk on you.

A "star" is symbolic of someone who dwells above the rest of us and shines in a dark world full of anonymity. But if the star's brightness fades, the name is "shuffled" to make room for contemporary famous names that will keep the tourists gawking.

The stars that God created last a little longer.

Oscar Wilde wrote, "We are all in the gutter, but some of us are looking at the stars" (*Lady Windermere's Fan*). Our life begins with the spark of youth, but it's easy to lose enthusiasm and become disillusioned by the pains and evils of this earth.

The distant stars seem to have a life of their own. These celestial bodies are unaffected by what happens on earth. It's as though we are looking into the eternality of another world. The Bible says of mankind:

> He has made everything beautiful in its time. Also He has put eternity in their hearts, except that no one can find out the work that God does from beginning to end. (Ecclesiastes 3:11)

God has put eternity in the heart of man. Animals lack the understanding of their existence—of "being," of considering the realities of life and death. Human beings exist with a yearning for the immortality that stars seem to suggest: "Twinkle, twinkle, little star, how I wonder what you are!"

The book of Jeremiah, written about 2,500 years ago, stated that there are so many stars, they *cannot* be numbered. On a clear night only about 3,000 can be seen with the naked eye, but with the advent of the telescope, wide-eyed gazers have discovered countless previously unknown stars. In the early 1600s, Galileo's homemade telescope enabled him to see an estimated 30,000 stars. Still, that's hardly *innumerable* as the Bible said. However, science is slowly catching up with the Scriptures. According to the European Space Agency,

> Astronomers estimate there are about 100 thousand million stars in the Milky Way alone. Outside that, there are millions upon millions of other galaxies also!

The Milky Way is the galaxy that contains our solar system. It is called the "milky" way because the stars cannot be individually distinguished by the naked eye. Up until the 1920s most astronomers thought that our galaxy contained all the stars in the universe. They had no idea that our galaxy is just one of billions of galaxies in the universe, each containing billions of stars.

The immensity of the universe is unfathomable—infinity larger than anyone imagined, and so big it has to be measured in billions of light-years:

> Astronomers have spotted the most distant star ever observed that is 9 billion light-years from Earth, a new study reported Monday.

> "For the first time ever we're seeing an individual normal star—not a supernova, not a gamma-ray burst, but a single, stable star—at a distance of 9 billion light-years," said Alex Filippenko, an astronomer at the University of California-Berkeley and co-author of the study.

> "This star is at least 100 times farther away than the next individual star we can study, except for supernova explosions," said the study's lead author, Patrick Kelly of the University of Minnesota.[21]

The Bible says, "As the host of heaven cannot be numbered, nor the sand of the sea measured . . ." (Jeremiah 33:22). The Bible correctly noted that there are so many they *couldn't* be numbered. Yet the universe is dwarfed by the infinite God who spoke it into existence:

> God, who at various times and in various ways spoke in time past to the fathers by the prophets, has in these last

days spoken to us by His Son, whom He has appointed heir of all things, through whom also He made the worlds. (Hebrews 1:1,2)

He *made* the worlds. Pondering this fact led the hymn writer to proclaim:

O LORD, my God, when I in awesome wonder
Consider all the worlds Thy hands have made,
I see the stars, I hear the rolling thunder,
Thy power throughout the universe displayed.[22]

The bigger the universe becomes in our understanding, the more in awe we should be of its Creator:

As of January 2009, we now know about some other really big stars. One is called Eta Carinae. It has a size about 800 times that of our Sun, a mass about 100 times that of our Sun, and is about 4,000,000 times brighter than our Sun. And, yet, we do not think it is the biggest! Recent observations of a star called VY Canus Majoris show that it has a size between 600 and 2100 times the size of our Sun! However, this star is only about 500,000 times brighter than our Sun and 30 or so times more massive than our Sun.[23]

Most of us would feel pity for someone who was so mentally deficient that he couldn't see the hand of the painter in any painting. But mankind's refusal to see the hand of the Creator in creation isn't a mental deficiency. It's a willful denial of the truth:

For ever since the creation of the world His invisible attributes, His eternal power and divine nature, have been clearly seen, being understood through His workmanship [all His creation, the wonderful things that He has made], so that they [who fail to believe and trust in Him] are without excuse and without defense. For even though they knew God [as the Creator], they did not honor Him as God or give thanks [for His wondrous creation]. On the contrary, they became worthless in their thinking [godless, with pointless reasonings, and silly speculations], and their foolish heart was darkened. (Romans 1:20,21, AMP)

In an article entitled "The Man Who Made Stars and Planets," *Discover* magazine said,

Thirty-five years ago, astrophysicist Alan Boss set off on a seemingly quixotic project: He wanted to figure out how planets form around stars. At the time astronomers knew little about the early history of our solar system and had no idea at all whether other stars even had planets. In essence, he wanted to build a model without knowing what he was modeling. Undeterred, Boss spent the next few decades working with the only example available—our own sun and planets—and making his best guesses...Each discovery has shown just how creative nature can be and has brought Boss a little closer to understanding the intricate process by which a swirling mass of gas and dust turns into a vibrant system of planets.[24]

Notice their view that "each discovery has shown just how creative nature can be." So it *wasn't* God who created everything in the beginning; it was nature. It made itself. How does that work "in the beginning"? How does nature make itself when it doesn't yet exist?

THE EYEBROW OF A DOG

The genius of God isn't only to be seen in the glory of the heavens. Once my understanding was enlightened through the new birth, I didn't even see a dog's eyebrow in the same light, let alone a star in the sky. Let's leave stars alone for a moment and think of things more down to earth, like the often taken for granted canine eyebrow:

> While most dog owners will recognize their pet's wagging tail as a sign of joy, they may also want to pay more attention to their animal's face the next time they walk in through the front door.
>
> Animal behavior experts have found the animals' emotions are betrayed by specific facial movements that can reveal whether your dog really is pleased to see you.
>
> Using high-speed cameras, the researchers tracked the changes in the faces of dogs in the moments they were reunited with their owners or when meeting a stranger for the first time.
>
> They found that the dogs tended to move their left eyebrow upwards around half a second after seeing their owner.[25]

Think about what's involved in its makeup. Each hair is rooted in the dog's flesh. It is preprogrammed by God to grow in a certain direction and to grow to a certain length and then stop.

Every hair! While it grows, it does so proportionally to the size of the dog. Then think about how He gave the dog the ability to react to his master. If he is happy, he shows it through individual hairs moving in unison. Just this tiny part of creation should make us raise our eyebrows at the magnificence of our Creator.

In one sense, the blind are fortunate. While they no doubt would give *anything* to have sight, they are free from a familiarity that is a curse for those who can see. We take the sky above us, stars, light, color, beauty, and a dog's eyebrow for granted. Most of us barely give a blue sky a second glance. We may think that it's nice to see blue heavens rather than dull and dreary clouds, but our mouth should be gaping in awe at the display of the big blue sky's breathtaking beauty. The Bible says that "the heavens *declare* the glory of God" (Psalm 19:1, emphasis added), but most of the unsaved and busy world hardly hear a whisper, because they are dull of hearing.

DEAF AND BLIND

If you're a Christian, let me talk to you about the love we should have for the lost. According to the Bible, they are blind (see 2 Corinthians 4:4). They have no idea where they are heading—that without the mercy of God in Christ, they are going to eventually stumble into Hell.

Our ministry received the following email from a believer named Greg:

> I thought of the gospel and Living Waters today, when my son came home for lunch. The apartment complex next to his in Greenwood, Indiana, had a fire yesterday. It was contained to

one building with 24 units. He said two guys were driving by when they noticed the fire on the second story (a 3-story building). They pulled over and started going through the building shouting "Fire!" and told everyone to get out. He said one of the guys was pounding on a door on the first story, yelling and told the resident to get out. She yelled back No! He pleaded with her, continually beating on the door saying, "This is for real!" She wouldn't come out, so he kicked the door in and got her out.

He kicked down the door, because he knew she didn't believe she was in danger. There's that word "believe" again. If you're not yet a believer, please think about what you're reading. Pointing out scientific facts in the Bible is simply an attempt to convince you that God is serious about sin, and that you are in terrible danger. Believe it, and you will do something about it. Stay in unbelief, and you will eventually lose you precious soul.

PREDICTABLE PLOT

There are certain old movies that I avoid watching. One of them is submarine films with that incessant "ping" noise running through them. The plot is predictable. You can be sure the oxygen will get thin, and sweaty men will then get agitated under the pressure and fight each other. And of course, water will begin to leak into the submarine.

A second nauseating movie plot is survivors who find themselves in a lifeboat with limited water and no food. In time they start eyeing one another for dinner.

Such a plot, however, isn't farfetched. There have been cases where people survived by becoming cannibals, sickening though the thought may be. How different their history would read if the boat they were in had been equipped with a simple fishing net, or a fishing line and bait.

When the Church sets aside the priority of fishing for men—something Jesus commands all His followers to do (Mark 1:17)—we tend to instead devour one another. Unity in mind and purposes comes with a genuine concern for the lost.

CRIME DOESN'T PAY

In 1940, MGM Studios produced a series of short films called *Crime Does Not Pay*, in which one episode dealt with shady companies selling fake merchandise. It is the true story of "Merchandise Distributors," who deal in stolen goods, and one of their customers named Carter & Collins Druggists.

One of the owners of the drugstore convinces his partner that they should purchase illegal goods, because of their low prices and high profits, to get them out of their financial difficulty. The lure of easy money to help the partner's family is too much to resist. But things go wrong and they end up getting caught. In those days, the criminals almost always got caught, and the lesson was that crime didn't pay.

However, things have changed since 1940. Nowadays lawlessness abounds and few end up in jail. Despite the sentiment, crime *does* pay. Less than 1 percent of rapists and 2 percent of those who commit robbery end up in jail. Just over 3 percent of those who assault someone are imprisoned.[26]

The sad fact is that evil is winning. A tsunami of corruption has engulfed the entire world. But the Day will come when Almighty God not only stops evil, but punishes the wicked. No one is getting away with anything. Sinners are just storing up wrath that will be revealed on what the Bible calls "the Day of the Lord." If they refuse to believe the gospel, on that Day the world will know that the only wage crime pays is death and Hell.

It is because of these sobering realities that we must never be guilty of having an uncaring heart toward the lost, or of devouring one other with criticism or gossip. Instead, we must run together to the unsaved and guide them to the light.

BACK TO THE STARS

The first recorded word that God spoke in the Bible was just three letters, yet its implications were phenomenal. In our English language, it was the word "Let." He used it to unlock light from the prison of non-existence. He spoke to something that didn't exist, and told it to come from nothing. And it was something by which we see all things, and as we have seen, it was something we tend to take for granted. It was light.

If you've ever wondered about the nature of light, here's a little light on the subject from *Cosmos* magazine:

> And so this is what light is: an electric field tied up with a magnetic field, flying through space.
>
> You can think of the two fields as dance partners, wrapped up in an eternal embrace. To keep self-generating, both electric and magnetic components need to stay in step. It takes two to tango.

Now we know that there is a whole spectrum of electro-magnetic waves, each distinguished by their wavelength. (You can think of the wavelength as the length of the dance step.)

At the short end, high-energy gamma rays can have a wavelength much smaller than a hydrogen atom, while at the long end, low-energy radiowaves can be as long as the planet Jupiter is wide. Visible light is a very thin slice of the electromagnetic spectrum, from wavelengths of about 400 to 700 billionths of a meter, about the width of an E. coli bacterium or about 1% the width of a human hair.[27]

If you're still in the dark as to the nature of light, after reading about dancing, Jupiter, *E. coli*, and human hair, perhaps the BBC can help:

Light is what allows us to understand the world we live in. Our language reflects this: after groping in the dark, we see the light and understanding dawns. Yet light is one of those things that we don't tend to understand. If you were to zoom in on a ray of light, what would you see? Sure, light travels incredibly fast, but what is it that's doing the travel-ing? Many of us would struggle to explain.

It doesn't have to be that way. Light certainly has puzzled the greatest minds for centuries, but landmark discoveries made over the last 150 years have robbed light of its mys-tery. We actually know, more or less, what it is.[28]

In reality, light is a mystery—like love and laughter, music and song. Definitions tend to be cold and illusive. It's like explaining the Mona Lisa as "paint and canvas."

Light is beautiful. Walk through your house and see the natural light pouring into certain rooms through windows. Look at how it is cut off by a wall, and yet notice how it blends gently from one room to another. Think of how its source came from 93,000,000 miles away at the breakneck speed of 186,000 miles *per second* from a burning star, so that you could have that blend of light and shadow in your home.

How could God make such a thing with the word "Let"? This wasn't like you and I turning a light on in a dark room and letting light manifest through the power of electricity. It was the *creation* of light from nothing. The fact is, we can't begin to know how this could happen. But what we do know it that when God says something, it happens. Nothing can resist His power. He said, "Let there be light; and there *was* light" (Genesis 1:3, emphasis added). One writer describes the nature of this light:

> The Bible student must deduce that the "light" of Genesis 1:3 was not that which subsequently (three days later) emanated from the sun, the moon, or the stars. The fiat of verse 14, "Let there be lights," expresses the same sort of creative activity—out of nothing came something by the command of God—that is affirmed in verse 3.
>
> Nor can it be argued legitimately that the sun, moon, and stars were "created" on the first day of the initial week, and then were simply made to "appear" on the fourth day, as

advocates of the Gap Theory have attempted to establish. There is no basis in the Hebrew text for that conclusion.[29]

THE EARLY BIRD AND GOLDILOCKS

One thing I find frustrating is the disconnect in my mind between God, the stars, and the rest of His creation. My mind connects His power to creation, but His genius seems distant. It takes a concerted effort to bring the two together.

Take for example early-morning birds. They "sing." We take it for granted that, like the rising sun, toast and coffee, it's part of our morning experience. What is happening doesn't register, perhaps because of the blindness that came with our sin nature. When I give concerted and serious thought to the singing birds, I almost lose my breath at the thought of the power of God. How could He program their DNA to sing? A songbird's singing parents didn't teach it the complexity of its songs. It didn't "learn" how to sing. God programmed it to be an intuitive skill. *As a young bird, it just started each morning singing.* It had the inclination to sing using the amazing vocal chords God had given it. And songbirds are just one extremely tiny part of this incredible thing we call "earth."

It does seem ironically appropriate that childish scientists who believe that we are simply a "lucky" planet call earth the "Goldilocks" planet:

"Many details as to why Earth is the only planet with liquid water in our solar system need to be worked out," said Diana Valencia, a graduate student in Earth and Planetary Sciences at Harvard University. "Certainly the distance to the sun has made it possible. A planet much farther in would receive too much energy from the sun, and a planet too far out would quickly freeze."

Our planet's Goldilocks-like "just right" location in the solar system has helped, as has its system of plate tectonics—the slip-sliding movements of Earth's crust that are thought to have created the planet's towering mountain ranges and plummeting ocean depths... Another "just-right" aspect of Earth is its size: If it was much smaller, it wouldn't be able to hold on to our precious atmosphere, but much larger and it might be a gas giant too hot for life.[30]

FISHING WITH SAM

I was riding my bike back from the ministry early one Saturday morning when I saw a well-dressed, elderly gentleman walking on the sidewalk. There are certain things that intimidate me, and one of them involves somebody who's a little older than me, who's well-dressed, walking on the sidewalk.

I ignored my fears, stopped, and gave the man one of our Ten Commandments coins. When he proved to be congenial, I asked if he thought there was an afterlife. He did. When I asked if he thought about it often he answered, "All the time." His name was Jack and he wasn't a Christian, but he said that his family was. So we went through the Commandments and into the cross. Jack was polite, and he was very pleased that I took the time to stop and speak with him. So was I.

One hundred yards further on the sidewalk, I saw a young

man who looked like a gang member. However, he was walking along with a Chihuahua on its leash. Gang members don't normally walk Chihuahuas; it's not a good image. That's unless you are super tough and really secure in your own thick skin.

I stopped and said, "Good morning. I have a gift for you." He walked over gingerly and I handed him the Ten Commandments coin, at the same time explaining what it was.

The young man's name is Renée. He wasn't a Christian, but he said he had family members who were inclined that way. As we went through the moral Law he said, "I'm dying anyway." I didn't want to get sidetracked, so I ignored what he said until we had been through the gospel. Then I went back and said, "You said that you were dying. What did you mean?"

He told me that he was waiting for a heart transplant and there was only a 10 percent chance of getting one. I told him that he looked healthy and I asked if I could pray for him. After we prayed, I gave him a number of Subway gift cards for him and his family. His eyes lit up with joy, and he said that I didn't realize how much all this meant to him. I then encouraged Renée to marry his girlfriend, get right with God, teach his children the way of salvation, and begin by reading the Gospel of John.

Because he said he was a reformed gang member who had done some really bad things in the past, I also explained the importance of not trusting in his own works. He had to trust entirely in the Savior. I said, "If you jump out of a plane with a parachute firmly strapped on, you don't flap your arms. You don't try to save yourself, but trust entirely in the parachute." He needed to trust entirely in the Savior and not look to his goodness to save him, because, like the rest of us, he didn't have any. He said that was a good analogy.

On the same morning I went out again with Sam and once again prayed that God would direct us and give us divine encounters.

The first person I spoke with said that he was a Christian, but he didn't read the Bible every day. He "tried" to. I explained to him that he didn't "try" to feed his stomach every day; he just *did* it. And that's what we should do with God's Word, if we profess to love Him. Then I shared the gospel with a young couple who listened intently and seemed very grateful that I had spoken to them. They both said, "Wow!" when I gave them a Subway gift card.

Off we went on the bike again, and about two hundred yards further along we saw a man who was walking alone. I say "we" because Sam is intently looking at everything like a hawk. I talk to him as we ride along, pointing out dogs, cats, and squirrels (things he's looking for) and people (things I'm looking for).

The person in front of us looked scary, but as I was approaching him I heard him say, "The dog is wearing sunglasses!" That was enough to get me to stop, and of course share the gospel with him. His name was Henry. When we got to the cross I could see tears well up in Henry's eyes. As drops began to roll down his face, I asked, "What's with the tears? Is it because you are sorry for your sins?" When he said it was, I said, "Let me pray for you." As we bowed together, I kept my eyes open and was amazed to see tears dropping onto the concrete path below like raindrops. It was heart-warming, and so refreshing to see genuine contrition. Now I was the one who was saying, "Wow!"

QUESTIONS TO CONSIDER

1. How many stars can be seen on a clear night?
2. How does understanding God's creative power help us to fear Him?
3. Are you ever afraid to let your light shine by sharing the gospel with the unsaved?
4. What do you fear most about evangelism?
5. What do scientific facts in the Bible do for your faith in God's Word (if they weren't there, would you feel the same)?
6. Why do some scientists refer to earth as "Goldilocks-like"?
7. Why is contrition (godly sorrow) so important in conversion? What part does it play? (See 2 Corinthians 7:10.)

3

THE LIFE IS IN THE BLOOD

I love witticisms, things like "If at first you don't succeed, don't try skydiving." I prefer a simpler version: "Don't try skydiving." There are too many deaths. Another is "Whatever you do, always give one hundred percent. Unless you're donating blood." This is because blood is essential for us to remain alive. It's the lifeblood of our body.

Every generation naturally considers itself modern. It thinks that it has the cutting-edge of technology and leads the way in fashion and music. But in time, its contemporary cutting-edge tastes become the blunt joke of the next generation. The quirky songs sung by groups with silly names like "Three Dog Night," the ugly cars, the poor quality of the movies, the horrible hairstyles, and the weird fashions of the past are ridiculed compared to what we have today. I'm a proud baby boomer, but I can't help feeling embarrassed by the crazy clothes and hairstyles of my generation.

Yet we thought we were *very* cool and that's all that mattered.

Ironically, I sometimes think that I would love to own an original Model-T Ford. But I know that after about ten minutes without power steering, air conditioning, air bags, and dual brakes, and feeling every back-breaking bump, I would long to be in my "modern" VW Beetle.

This generation thinks that we have come a long way medically. While I'm grateful for skillful doctors, for anesthesia and painkillers, there are thousands of diseases that still outwit us, and "cures" that have side effects that are worse than the disease. After hundreds of years of battling cancer, we are not winning the war, with almost ten million cancer deaths per year.[31] Modern isn't always good.

Up until two hundred years ago, the *modern* practice was to "bleed" sick people, and many died because of it. It was cutting-edge medicine, but it was wrong. When you lose your blood, you lose your life.

When George Washington became deathly sick, doctors thought that bloodletting would help. It certainly didn't:

> On December 13, 1799, George Washington awoke with a bad sore throat and began to decline rapidly. A proponent of bloodletting, he asked to be bled the next day, and physicians drained an estimated 5 to 7 pints in less than 16 hours. Despite their best efforts, Washington died on December 17, leading to speculation that excessive blood loss contributed to his demise. Bloodletting has also been implicated in the death of Charles II, who was bled from the arm and neck after suffering a seizure in 1685.[32]

Nowadays, we know that sick people often *need* blood and we give them transfusions. Rather than removing it, we replace it because the life of the flesh is in the blood.

Leviticus 17:11, written 3,500 years ago, declared that blood is essential for life: "For the life of the flesh is in the blood."

THE WARMTH OF THE FLESH

Do you ever think about what it is that keeps your body nice and warm? While there are external influences, the main internal influence is heat from food that's carried to your body's extremities by your blood. We are called *warm-blooded* creatures, because our blood is warm.

Beneath your soft flesh is a gushing river of pressurized and heated blood-red blood, racing through an incredibly intricate plumbing system. Ugh. It's not a pleasant thought, unless you are some sort of biology geek who actually *enjoyed* cutting up dead worms in school.

I have a friend who can't look into the mirror when he brushes his teeth, because the thought of saliva makes him feel sick. Many feel the same about blood. Seeing it makes them almost faint, and the very thought that a red river is gushing through us is not something that many of us like to meditate on.

Like it or not, if you are an adult human being, you are a container of more than a gallon of thick oozing blood, which makes up just over 7 percent of your total body weight. Your heart is an amazing blood-pump made of muscle, and is slightly larger than your fist. It continuously pumps blood through the circulatory system, beating around 100,000 times and pumping a swimming pool of about 2,000 gallons of blood each day. In an average life-time, the heart beats over 2.5 billion times.

Think of what God must be like, to create such a thing as the human heart. Once a tiny glimpse enters your mind and you are able wrap your thoughts around His incredible power, think of the heart of the elephant, the giraffe, the lion, the whale, and the hum-mingbird. How could He think of such things? From where did He obtain the materials? How could all the essential components come together and support life? Suddenly, these thoughts become too much for our minds. Like a failing champion weightlifter, we grow overwhelmed, and we drop the thought because it becomes too heavy for us. We say with the psalmist, "Such knowledge is too wonderful for me; it is high, I cannot attain it" (Psalm 139:6).

The blood flow is as essential to our body as air is to our lungs. It's the blood that works hand-in-hand with our lungs—through an independent fully automated system that carries oxygen to the different parts of our body.

While we may not faint at the sight, most of us are alarmed when we see any blood. It's red, and intuitive alarm bells go off when we see that color. We use the alarming color of blood-red for the color of stop signs, fire alarms, and fire engines, because of this reaction.

Again, *force* yourself to think of God's super-amazingly cre-ative mind in coming up with this system, and of His ability to make His imaginative mind a reality. Think about how we were conceived in the womb of our mother, thanks to our father. In just a few short weeks, our heart, blood, and the necessary sys-tem to accommodate and facilitate it all manifest from the DNA within our tiny bodies.

The blood was manufactured in the bone marrow—in bones that didn't exist until they appeared out of nowhere. Soft skin covered us to keep it all in, and a heart appeared to pump our blood around to keep us alive, even though our lungs at that time weren't breathing air—until our first breath came the moment we slipped outside of the womb.

Can you imagine how many doctors and scientists would have to work together to figure out how to make just one living baby? If they started with the raw materials, how long would it take them to create the computer-center brain, to work in harmony with eyes, legs, hands, feet, nerves, bones, muscles, and all the countless other intricate interrelated parts to make this thing work? But then there's a problem, a big one—how to make a soul. The body is just an elaborate inanimate pumping machine until the soul enters to make what we call "life" a reality.

> As you do not know what is the way of the wind, or how
> the bones grow in the womb of her who is with child, so
> you do not know the works of God who makes everything.
> (Ecclesiastes 11:5)

Of course, a living human body could never be made by man. Not in a million years. We can't make even one minuscule drop of warm blood from nothing.

Yet we are told that man *can* make blood, in an article titled "Scientists Create Artificial Blood That Can Be Produced On An Industrial Scale: A Limitless Supply Of Blood?":

> With this new method, scientists hope they'll produce a sort
> of "limitless" supply of type-O red blood cells, free of diseases

and able to be transfused into any patient. Blood transfusions are used to replace lost blood after an injury or surgery. According to the National Institutes of Health, every year five million Americans require blood transfusions.

Through the use of pluripotent stem cells—regular cells removed from the human body and then transformed into stem cells—Turner and his team of researchers were able to create blood type O red blood cells. The technique will be tested in live humans for the first time, in a trial running through 2016 or 2017. In the experiments, researchers will test the artificial blood on people who have thalassaemia, a blood disorder that requires several transfusions.[33]

Man cheats by using *God's* materials, and takes the glory for what he thinks he creates.

May God open our blind eyes so that we can get a tiny glimpse of Who and what He is. Such revelations of His creative power will open the grand doors of worship, explode our faith, and help us to control tormenting fears and fear Him as we should.

FISHING WITH SAM

It was a Thursday afternoon in late April 2018. The sun felt hot, but the air was nice and cool as Sam and I rode the bike.

Once again strangers waved and called out when they saw a dog wearing sunglasses. As I turned into the local park I saw two gentlemen in their early thirties walking toward me on a path, led by a small white dog. They had obviously been playing basketball because they looked hot and sweaty, making me think they wouldn't want to stop and talk. I also had the thought that I didn't want another dog brought into the equation, because barking would certainly bring confusion. However, before I could get a word in, the gentleman on my left called out, "Wow! That's amazing. I was thinking of making one of those for my dog last night. Could you stop and let me see how you did that?"

For the next few moments I explained to him how I had made the platform for Sam, how it was secured to the bike, and how Sam was held in with his own seatbelt. I then gave both of them Ten Commandment coins and explained to Rick and Mario what they were. Rick told me he was a Catholic.

When I asked Rick if he would let me interview them on-camera, he said that would be fine, but when his dog suddenly started barking, he changed his mind. I pleaded with him to stay and allow me talk to him off-camera for three or four minutes, so he stayed and we went through the Commandments into the gospel. I thanked them both for staying and listening to me, told them how important it was to get right with God, and gave both of them a gift card.

As they walked away, I could see them talking together. Then Rick turned around and said, "There's no such thing as coincidence, right?" I said, "Right!" and smiled.

EXERCISING RICHARD

I had ridden past a man as he was walking in the other direction. He was about thirty yards behind me when I called out that I had a gift for him. He stopped in his tracks but was hesitant to walk toward me, so I turned my bike around, approached him, and gave him a Ten Commandments coin explaining what it was.

He said that he didn't have time to talk because he was out doing his afternoon exercise. I asked if I could walk with him, and he said that I could. I then introduced myself and as we walked along I asked him if he believed there was an afterlife. Richard said that he did, but when we went through the Commandments he, like everyone else, he proved to be guilty of breaking them. That's when he said that he didn't want to talk anymore.

I apologized for offending him, said that I had a parting gift before I left, and gave him a gift card. He was clearly taken aback and immediately began asking me questions. For the next fifteen to twenty minutes he had question after question, such as which way was the right way, and about other religions. During this time, I explained that the reason he wanted to get away from me was because of his guilt. We naturally love the darkness and hate the light, and when the light comes on, we move away from it and want to go back to the darkness. I could see his eyes processing the information. Richard even accepted a signed book.

That little gift card put the wisdom of Scripture into practice: "For this is the will of God, that by doing good you may put to silence the ignorance of foolish men" (1 Peter 2:15).

QUESTIONS TO CONSIDER

1. Until how recently did doctors practice bloodletting? Why did doctors do this?

2. What does the sight of blood do to you? Have you ever seriously cut yourself?

3. Do you ever feel the weight of thought as you consider the power of God?

4. How many times does your heart beat each day?

5. What adjective would you use to describe God?

6. If you're a Christian, do you ever share the gospel with strangers?

7. What is your greatest fear in evangelism?

4

THE EARTH IS ROUND

Around the World in Eighty Days is one of my favorite movies. It has everything a good movie needs—great character development, romance, adventure, excellent theme music, humor, tension, and intrigue. It was based on Jules Verne's book of the same name, published in 1873.

Things have sped up since those days. According to *Popular Mechanics*:

> In the last hundred years, the world has become drastically more accessible. It's difficult to imagine in the age of jet planes, but not long ago, getting from one side of the world to the other was a long and arduous process. Not to mention circling the world entirely. When Magellan's crew became the first people to do so in 1521, the journey took three years, and most of the crew, including Magellan, died on the way.

But what's the very fastest we can circumnavigate the globe today? ... Essentially, the answer depends on the rules of the game. The record for circumnavigating the world within our own atmosphere was set back in 1992 by Air France, who made the trip in the Concorde in a little under 33 hours. But once you get into outer space, much faster times become possible. The astronauts on the International Space Station circle the Earth every 92 minutes. Elon Musk says his rockets will one day be able to take passengers anywhere on the planet in under an hour. But until then, we're stuck with air travel.[34]

Those who discount the authority of the Bible say that we don't need the Scriptures to tell us the shape of our globe. In an article by the BBC titled "We have known that Earth is round for over 2,000 years," the author pointed to the Greeks and stated,

Long before anyone circumnavigated the globe or went into space, the ancient Greeks had figured out that the Earth is ball-shaped, rather than flat.[35]

Actually, it's been much longer than that. The Scriptures themselves tell us that the earth is round:

It is He who sits above the circle of the earth. (Isaiah 40:22)

The word translated "circle" here is the Hebrew word *chuwg*, which is also translated "circuit" or "compass," depending on the context. That is, it indicates something spherical, rounded like a ball, or arched—not something that is flat or square. The book of Isaiah was written around 700 BC. This is at least 300 years before Aristotle suggested, in his book *On the Heavens*, that the earth might be a sphere. He did this by watching masts of ships sink down over the horizon and from the studies of the moon during an eclipse. He perceptively noted the shadow of the earth on the moon revealed that the earth was curved. It was another 2,000 years later, at a time when many believed that the earth was flat, that the Scriptures inspired Christopher Columbus to sail around the world.

In a book titled *Christopher Columbus: His Life and Discovery in the Light of His Prophecies*, by Kay Brigham, the following quote from Columbus is noted:

At this time I have seen and put in study to look into all the Scriptures, cosmography, histories, chronicles and philosophy and other arts, which our Lord opened to my understanding (I could sense his hand upon me), so that it became clear to me that it was feasible to navigate from here to the Indies; and he unlocked within me the determination to execute the idea. And I came to your Highnesses with this ardor. All those who heard about my enterprise rejected it with laughter, scoffing at me. Neither the sciences which I mentioned above, nor the authoritative citations from them, were of any avail. In only your Highnesses remained faith and constancy. Who doubts that this illumination was from the Holy Spirit? I attest that he (the Spirit), with marvelous rays of light, consoled me through the holy and sacred Scriptures ... encouraging me to proceed, and, continually, without ceasing for a moment, they inflame me with a sense of great urgency ...

I am the worst of sinners. The pity and mercy of our Lord have completely covered me whenever I have called (on him) for them. I have found the sweetest consolation in casting away all my anxiety, so as to contemplate his marvelous presence.

I have already said that for the execution of the enterprise of the Indies, neither reason, nor mathematics, nor world maps were profitable to me; rather the prophecy of Isaiah was completely fulfilled.[36]

In his book *Sails of Hope*, Simon Wiesenthal noted about Columbus' own writings:

That religious elements played a great part in Columbus's thoughts and actions is evident from all his writings. It may come as something of a surprise to us that his concept of sailing west to reach the Indies was less the result of geographical theories than of his faith in certain Biblical texts— specifically the Book of Isaiah.[37]

Yet, despite what the Scriptures and science say, unbelievably there are still some today who believe that the earth is flat. According to the Flat Earth Society:

The earth is surrounded on all sides by an ice wall that holds the oceans back. This ice wall is what explorers have named Antarctica. Beyond the ice wall is a topic of great interest to the Flat Earth Society. To our knowledge, no one has been very far past the ice wall and returned to tell of their journey. What we do know is that it encircles the earth and serves to hold in our oceans and helps protect us from whatever lies beyond.[38]

What is even harder to believe is that among some professing Christians there is a growing number who have the mistaken belief that the earth is flat. While it's embarrassing to have to rebut such an absurdity, it is interesting to understand how we know that the earth is round.

As we have seen earlier, Aristotle came to believe that the earth is round by watching the moon, and seeing the shadow of the earth on its surface. The shadow curves as it moves across the moon showing us that the earth is round and, beyond a shadow of a doubt, not flat.

We have also seen that he watched ships come up and go down over the horizon. They didn't instantly disappear as they fell off the edge of the earth, as would have happened if the earth were flat.

Aristotle also noticed that the stars in Egypt were different than the stars he saw in other places on the earth. He said, "There are stars in Egypt and . . . Cypress which are not seen in the northerly regions." If the earth were flat, everyone on the earth would see the same stars. But they don't. The stars in the southern hemisphere are different from those in the northern hemisphere. This shows us that the earth is not flat.

Another proof that the earth is round is the fact that we can see much further from the window of a plane at 30,000 feet than we can see from the window of a building that is 1,000 feet high. The reason we can see further is that we are looking across the curvature of the earth. This wouldn't be the case if it were flat and again shows us that the earth is round. The BBC article continues:

> Another Greek thinker and mathematician, Eratosthenes, went further and managed to measure the Earth's circumference. He discovered that at noon in one Egyptian city, the Sun was directly overhead, whereas in a different city the Sun did not rise quite so high. Eratosthenes knew the distance between the two cities, measured how high in the sky the Sun rose to in each at the same time, then did some trigonometry. His method was crude, but his answer was in the right ballpark.
>
> The fact that Earth is round has been common knowledge, at least among the educated and powerful, ever since.
>
> More recently, people have gone all the way round the Earth. The Portuguese explorer Ferdinand Magellan famously circumnavigated the Earth from 1519 to 1522, which would have been even more difficult if it had had an edge.
>
> But long before Magellan, it was obvious to observant sailors that the Earth is round. If you sail towards something tall, like a mountain, you will see the top of it appearing over the horizon before the rest of it.[39]

Nowadays we also have many thousands of photos and video of the earth from space and none of them show us a flat earth. It is round. Just like the Bible says.

A BALL COVERED BY WATER

Most contemporary scientists don't thank God for creating this amazing earth. Instead they are amazed at how "lucky" we are that water appeared on its surface. This is because humanity is nothing but a very dead duck without water. We certainly are "lucky."

We are lucky that the sun is positioned at 93,000,000 miles because any closer and we're a cooked goose. Any further away and we're a frozen turkey. We're lucky that gravity had worked itself out so we could exist.

We sure are lucky that there was food on the earth because without it we would have starved. It's also lucky that we had an appetite, a taste for food, teeth to chew, an esophagus to swallow, saliva to lubricate, a stomach to send it to, acids to break it down and send it into our lucky blood to give us energy.

A recent *Newsweek* article explained how water luckily could have made it to earth. It was titled "Scientists Used a Super Powerful Cannon to Show How Asteroids Can Carry Water Between Worlds":

> The Earth's nickname, "the Blue Marble," comes from being covered with water—but where did that water come from? It's one of science's biggest mysteries, and plenty of ink has been spilled trying to design scenarios that make sense.[40]

But nothing makes sense if you look to Lady Luck and leave God out if the equation. If water did arrive on the earth on asteroids, where did it come from and how did it get on the asteroids?

How was it that it miraculously had the composition of water? Water is extremely complex:

> A water molecule consists of three atoms: an oxygen atom and two hydrogen atoms, which are bond together like little magnets. The atoms consist of matter that has a nucleus in the center.
>
> The difference between atoms is expressed by atomic numbers. The atomic number of an atom depends on the number of protons in the nucleus of the atom. Protons are small positively charged particles. Hydrogen has one proton in the nucleus and oxygen has eight. There are also uncharged particles in the nucleus, called neutrons.
>
> Next to protons and neutrons, atoms also consist of negatively charged electrons, which can be found in the electron cloud around the nucleus. The number of electrons in an atom equals the number of protons in the nucleus. The attraction between the protons and electrons is what keeps an atom together.[41]

Water may sound simple—H_2O—but if it were, we would be able to create it from nothing. But we can't. We don't have a clue how to create one drip or even a drop, let alone an ocean, without using the building blocks that God provided. So how did all of the earth's water get into asteroids that were lucky enough to be shooting in the right direction toward the earth, hit it, and conveniently leave the deposit of enough water to fill our oceans?

Human beings weren't the only lucky ones. Perhaps some lucky fish also hitchhiked their way across the universe in that water, survived the impact, and evolved into male and female to make more fish (makes just as much sense). The *Newsweek* article continues:

> But there's another approach: dreaming up experiments that could demonstrate how those scenarios might have played out. A new attempt to mimic water's arrival on Earth made use of an exotic tool—an incredibly powerful cannon that parodies an asteroid impacting Earth. The results are published in the journal *Science Advances.*

> Models had suggested that water may have arrived on Earth through impacts by a group of objects called carbonaceous chondrites—meteorites that break off an asteroid full of water and fall to Earth.[42]

Where would such water-filled asteroids come from? But that question doesn't seem to matter with this experiment. What matters is whether or not the water would have evaporated during the incredibly hot conditions upon impact:

> So the team turned to NASA's Vertical Gun Range in California, which was designed to produce small replicas of the sort of high-power collisions that are common in space. The device is powerful enough to shoot a marble at speeds of more than 11,000 miles per hour, which is still only about half the speed of the slowest meteorite impacts.

> The scientists made small marbles with the same recipe as the wet carbonaceous chondrites, then used the high-power cannon to shoot it into a very dry rocky surface. The result was a mess of melted and re-hardened rock.[43]

After experimenting, researchers admit that two-thirds of the water would be lost during impact, yet they *have faith* that the experiment was successful:

> Scientists *believe* that early in Earth's life, it would have been pummeled with one after another of these impacts—and the new evidence *suggests* that those impacts *could* add up to the watery world we love so much (emphasis added).[44]

The theory is that the earth was bombarded with water-filled asteroids for 100,000,000 years, and that gave us what we have on earth today. In National Geographic's documentary *One Strange Rock*, astronaut Nicole Stott declares, "So we can thank our lucky stars, I suppose, that the seed that started earth was in the right place for water to exist in its three states."

So there you have it—the possible origin of fresh water, salt water, happy fish and thirsty people, waterfalls, rain clouds, lakes, and oceans. And all of this is clinging to the surface of a lucky earth, spinning through space at a breakneck speed, for no rhyme or reason.

FISHING WITH SAM

It was a Friday morning and we were expecting a 190-pound canopy to be delivered that afternoon. But an early-bird phone-call came at seven in the morning, and the deliveryman said they would be there in twenty minutes. I frantically jumped out of bed, took a quick shower, got dressed, ran downstairs, and there they were. Two guys, Ulysses and Mario, carrying the big canopy.

I gave them each a book that I had written, thanked them for the delivery, and as suddenly as they came, they were gone.

I felt sick. If only I had said, "Guys, can I talk to you for three minutes? Do you think there is an afterlife?" But I didn't; I chickened out. I am the chief of chickens. And the reason I chickened out was that I didn't have a plan. I didn't bother to give any forethought to their visit. I didn't pray for them before they arrived and I didn't think to myself, "I'm going to do this!"

If you want to conquer your fears, make sure you have a plan. Lift yourself above your fears or they will lift themselves above you. Overcome or be overcome. Make sure you know what you are going to do and what you're going to say.

That Friday afternoon I was fishing with Sam when I saw a lone person sitting on a seat in the park. I rode my bike across the grass and stopped about ten feet from the person. It was only then that I saw it was young lady, perhaps in her mid-twenties, listening to music and playing with her iPhone. When I greeted her she didn't look up. It was only when I yelled, "Hello!" that she took any notice. Then I gave her a Ten Commandments coin and asked if she thought there's an afterlife. She did, but it wasn't "eternal life"—she believed everyone was going to go to sleep, and then be resurrected. When I asked if she was a Jehovah's Witness, she smiled and said she was.

Her name was Wednesday, and even though she didn't want to go on camera, she said that I could speak to her for a few moments.

As usual with Jehovah's Witnesses, she thought she was a good person, so I gave her a challenging scenario. I said that there was a knife in my back and I've got three minutes to live—"How can I enter the Kingdom?" I have found that this scenario is an effective way of revealing if somebody is trusting in their own righteousness to save them, or in God's mercy. She couldn't tell me what I should do to be saved.

After going through the Commandments, I said the moral Law nails us to the cross. It condemns us, just like the thief on the cross. Because he was nailed, there was nothing he could do but turn to Jesus, and that's what we have to do to be saved. We can't go anywhere and we can't do anything. Only faith in Jesus can save us.

Minutes after I spoke with Wednesday on that Friday, two of my neighbors (who were out for a regular walk) walked up to me and we began chatting about Sam and his sunglasses. I gave them a coin and asked them about the afterlife. They were Buddhists, and they politely listened as I shared the gospel. I normally find it a little frightening to witness to neighbors, because you don't want to upset those who live in close proximity. But I'm glad I did on that day.

DOOR KNOCKER

One of our neighboring families are Jehovah's Witnesses, to whom we had given gifts and prayed nightly for years.

One day there was a knock on our door. A young lady introduced herself as being the married daughter of the Jehovah's Witness family. She had an egg carton in her hand and asked if she could buy $10 worth of our eggs. Her family was away and she knew that we often gave them eggs from our chicken coop. I told her that I would love to give her some.

I went and got some out of the refrigerator, then gave them to her along with a book that I'd written called *How to Battle Depression and Suicidal Thoughts*. As I gave it to her, I said that she may not suffer from depression and suicidal thoughts herself, but she might know someone who did. She looked at the book, then back at me with tears in her eyes, and almost collapsed. She said that she had been having severe depression, serious thoughts of suicide, and had been seeing a psychiatrist.

We sat down on the doorstep, and I asked her if the psychiatrist told her that she had a mental disease. She said he had. I said that she didn't, and that it was only thirty or forty years ago that psychiatry decided to classify depression as being a mental disease—and that opened the door for the multi-billion industry of prescription drugs. I told her that it was normal to be depressed because life *is* deeply depressing, especially because of the fact that we are all going to die.

When I asked if she was a Jehovah's Witness, she said, "Kind of." I told her I was going to share the gospel with her from the Bible, and I took her through the Commandments then asked why it was that Jesus died on the cross. She said it was so that we could eventually gain perfection. I told her that idea was Jehovah's Witness doctrine, but that the Bible tells us Jesus died so we might be instantly made morally perfect by the grace of God, totally cleansed of sin and made righteous.

I gave her some helpful material and a Subway gift card and prayed with her on the doorstep. She said that her coming to our house hadn't been about eggs, but that God had brought her over that day.

QUESTIONS TO CONSIDER

1. Describe where and how the Bible says the earth is round.

2. Why is this not referring to a flat disk?

3. How did Aristotle come to the conclusion that the earth is round?

4. If I believed that the earth is flat, why should I keep that thought to myself?

5. What inspired Christopher Columbus to sail around the world?

6. Do you believe that humans are a lucky accident or that we are created by God?

7. What should we do to prepare to witness to someone?

5

THE SCIENCE OF OCEANOGRAPHY

I grew up being able to see the ocean from my bedroom. The beach was a mere one hundred yards away, so my summers were soaked in salt water. One of the greatest gifts my parents gave me was a large inflated tractor tire tube. I would roll it to the beach and spend carefree hours floating on it, diving off it and bouncing on endless waves. As I grew older, I threw myself into surfing and spent even longer hours in the ocean.

The ocean not only gives us the wonderful pleasures of water sports such as surfing, skiing, swimming, boating, diving, etc., it feeds us with an amazing variety of delicious fish. Life on earth would not be the same without the five big oceans that surround us.

Matthew Maury is considered to be the father of oceanography. He noticed the expression "paths of the sea" in Psalm 8:8 (written 2,800 years ago) and said, "If God said there are paths in the sea, I am going to find them." Maury then had a notion, took God at His Word, and went looking for these paths. And we are indebted to his discovery of the warm and cold continental currents. His vital book on oceanography was a basic text on the subject and is still in print today.

> Born in Spotsylvania County, Virginia, in 1806, Maury was surrounded in childhood and youth by those whose lives were enriched by a deep and abiding respect for the Bible as the Word of God.

> Maury grew to have a similar trust in the revealed Word, a trust which was to make him one of America's greatest creationist scientists. Throughout his life he never disguised the relationship he saw between the creation and the Creator, between science and scripture.[45]

Matthew Maury took the time to study old ships' logs, and he used these to compile charts of the ocean-wind and sea currents. In an effort to study the speed and direction of ocean currents he released weighted bottles that were known as "drift bottles." These bottles floated just below the surface and therefore were not affected by wind. Instructions were placed into each bottle, asking anyone who found one washed up on shore to return it. After studying the location and date on each of the bottles, Maury was able to create his charts of the ocean currents—the "paths" of the seas—which greatly aided the science of marine navigation.

> It has been reserved for one of our own countrymen to discover the paths of the sea; to map the tracks of the winds; to shorten sailing time to California thirty days, to Australia twenty, and to Rio Janeiro ten. He has communed with the

spirit of the sea earnestly and lovingly; and while it shouted to others in thunder peals of omnipotence, and majesty, and eternity, it came and whispered to him in gentle and soothing tones of divine beneficence, wisdom, love. The American Franklin drew the lightning from heaven; the American Morse sent it as an errand-boy along the oscillating wire; and now again American genius stands confessed in high superiority, as Maury tells us "whence the wind cometh and whither it goeth," and then declares that long, long ago the Bible announced the same teachings.

He has shown us that the most exquisite proofs of perfect design and infinite skill are manifested in ocean laws. Take the Gulf Stream. Here we have a river in the sea, "which in the severest drouths never fails, in the mightiest floods never overflows; with banks and bottom of cold water, while the current is of warm." It flows ceaselessly from the Gulf of Mexico to the Arctic Seas. It has a current more rapid than the Mississippi or Amazon. Some of our American writers supposed this stream was caused by the Mississippi river, which had accumulated so much western American force of character, that, entering the ocean through the Gulf, it pushed boldly on, holding tenaciously together on the ground that "the union must be preserved, and refusing to submit to any interference from Neptune till it paid its homage to Terminus in the Arctic Sea, and, in a quiet, respectable, and eminently American manner, froze up!"[46]

It's interesting to ask those who say there's no evidence of a worldwide flood why it is that 70 percent of the earth's surface is covered with water. Ask them where it came from, and most don't know. They've never thought about it. Could it be that they are the leftover puddle from the flood?

Earth has a big puddle of around 326 million trillion gallons of water. But only about 3 percent of that is freshwater, and more than two-thirds of that is locked up in ice caps and glaciers.

Aside from the water that exists in ice form, there is also the staggering amount of water that exists beneath the Earth's surface. If you were to gather all the Earth's fresh water together as a single mass...it is estimated that it would measure some 1,386 million cubic kilometers (km³) in volume.[47]

Think about it: Matthew Maury had faith that the Bible was the Creator's instruction Book to humanity. When he saw the expression "paths of the sea" in Psalm 8:8, he trusted that it wasn't a mere metaphor written by the pen of a man. That's the wonderful thing about the Bible—we can trust *every* word. It has instructions for every walk of life telling us what we should and shouldn't do.

But the world thinks it knows better. Maury said,

Astronomy ignores the existence of man; physical geography confesses that existence, and is based on the Biblical doctrine "that the earth was made for man." Upon no other theory can it be studied—upon no other theory can its phenomena be reconciled...

I have been blamed by men of science, both in this country and in England, for quoting the Bible in confirmation of the doctrines of physical geography. The Bible, they say, was not written for scientific purposes, and is therefore of no authority in matters of science. I beg pardon! The Bible is authority for everything it touches. What would you think of the historian who should refuse to consult the historical records of the Bible, because the Bible was not written for the purposes of history? The Bible is true and science is true, and therefore each, if truly read, but proves the truth of the other. The agents in the physical economy of our planet are ministers of Him who made both it and the Bible. The records which He has chosen to make through the agency of these ministers of His upon the crust of the earth are as true as the records which, by the hands of His prophets and servants, He has been pleased to make in the Book of Life.[48]

The following is a lengthy but wonderful letter, written by Maury in 1855, showing his love for and faith in the Scriptures:

The Bible and Science

Observatory, Washington, Jan. 22, 1855

Your letter revived pleasant remembrances. Your questions are themes. It would require volumes to contain the answers to them.

You ask about the "harmony of science and revelation," and wish to know if I find distinct traces in the Old Testament of scientific knowledge, and in the Bible any knowledge of the winds and ocean currents. Yes, knowledge the most correct and reliable.

Canst thou bind the sweet influences of the Pleiades? It is a curious fact, that the revelations of science have led astronomers of our own day to the discovery, that the sun is not the dead centre of motion around which comets sweep and planets whirl, but that it, with its splendid retinue of worlds and satellites, is revolving through space at the rate of millions of miles in a year, and in obedience to some influence situated precisely in the direction of the star Alcyon, one of the Pleiades. We do not know how far off in the immensities of space that centre of revolving cycles and epicycles may be, nor have our oldest observers or nicest instruments been able to tell us how far off in the skies that beautiful cluster of stars is hung "whose influences man can never bind." In this question alone, and the answer to it, are involved both the recognition and the exposition of the whole theory of gravitation.

Science taught that the world was round; but potentates pronounced the belief heretical, notwithstanding the Psalmist, while apostrophizing the works of creation in one of his sublime moods of inspiration, "when prophets spake as they were moved," had called the world "the round world," and "bade it rejoice."

You remember when Galileo was in prison a pump-maker came to him with his difficulties, because his pump would not lift water higher than thirty-two feet. The old philosopher thought it was because the atmosphere would not press the water up any higher; but the hand of persecution was upon him, and he was afraid to say the air had weight. Now, had he looked to the science of the Bible, he would have discovered that the "perfect man of Uz," moved by inspiration, had proclaimed the fact thousands of years before—"He maketh weight for the wind." Job is very learned, and his speeches abound in scientific lore. The persecutors of the old astronomers would also have been wiser and far more just had they paid more attention to this wonderful book, for there they would have learned that He "stretcheth out the north over the empty place, and hangeth the earth upon nothing."

Here is another proof that Job was familiar with the laws of gravitation, for he knew how the world was held in its place; and as for "the empty place" in the sky, Sir John Herschel has been sounding the heavens with his powerful telescope, and gauging the stars; and where do you think he found the most barren part—"the empty places" of the sky? In the north, precisely where Job told Bildad, the Shuhite, the empty place was stretched out. It is there where comets most delight to roam and hide themselves in emptiness.

I pass by the history of creation as it is written on the tablets of the rocks and in the Book of Revelation, because the question has been discussed so much and so often, that you, no doubt, are familiar with the whole subject. In both the order of creation is the same. First, the plants to afford subsistence, and then the animals...

I will, however, before proceeding further, ask pardon for mentioning a rule of conduct which I have adopted in order to make progress with these physical researches, which have occupied so much of my time and so many of my thoughts. The rule is, never to forget who is the Author of the great volume which Nature spreads out before us, and always to remember that the same Being is the Author of the book which revelation holds up to us, and though the two works are entirely different, their records are equally true, and when they bear upon the same point, as now and then they do, it is as impossible that they should contradict each other as it is that either should contradict itself. If the two cannot be reconciled, the fault is ours, and is because, in our blindness and weakness, we have not been able to interpret aright either the one or the other, or both.

Solomon, in a single verse, describes the circulation of the atmosphere as actual observation is now showing it to be. That it has its laws, and is obedient to order as the heavenly host in their movements, we infer from the facts announced by him, and which contain the essence of volumes by other men. "All the rivers run into the sea, yet the sea is not full;" "Into the place from whence the rivers come, thither they return again."

To investigate the laws which govern the winds and rule the sea is one of the most profitable and beautiful occupations that a man—an improving, progressive man—can have. Decked with stars as the sky is, the field of astronomy affords no subjects of contemplation more ennobling, more sublime, or more profitable than those which we may find in the air and the sea. When we regard these from certain points of view, they present the appearance of wayward things, obedient to no law, but fickle in their movements, and subject only to chance.

Yet, when we go as truth-loving, knowledge-seeking explorers, and knock at their secret chambers, and devoutly ask what are the laws which govern them, we are taught, in terms the most impressive, that "when the morning stars sang together, the waves also lifted up their voice," and the winds, too, "joined in the mighty anthem."

And as the discovery advances, we find the mark of order in the sea and in the air that is in tune with the "music of the spheres," and the conviction is forced upon us that the laws of all are nothing else but perfect harmony.

Yours respectfully,

M. F. Maury, Lieut. U.S. Navy[49]

MIND-BLOWING SCIENCE

I once saw a movie called *Being There*, in which Peter Sellers played a simple gardener at a townhouse in Washington, DC. When he lost his job, he was forced to vacate his home, and while wandering the streets, he encountered a business mogul who wrongly assumed him to be a fellow upper-class gentleman. In time he was ushered into high society.

He would say things like, "As long as the roots are not severed, all is well," and those around him mistakenly thought he was speaking deep philosophy. They would read into his words things that weren't there. In time, his reputation had him advising presidents, who also read into his words things that weren't there.

So it was with famed physicist and atheist Stephen Hawking. It wasn't his fault. When he spoke, a lost and blind world heard deep philosophy and latched onto his words as if they were gospel.

One awe-inspired and wide-eyed reporter said, "Let Stephen Hawking blow your mind with what happened before the Big Bang."[50]

Here are Stephen's mind-blowing words:

The boundary condition of the universe . . . is that it has no boundary.

That is deep. What does he mean "the universe has no boundary"? One reporter interprets what the deep-thinking gardener must be saying:

In other words, there is no time before time began as time was always there.[51]

That *is* profound. Time had no beginning, but it's always been there. Like the sun is hot, but it's cold. The roots are deep.

Hawking also told physicist Neil deGrasse Tyson that time was there, but it was in a "bent" state. What did he mean by "bent" time? The reporter interprets for us:

It was distorted along another dimension—always getting fractionally closer to, but never becoming, nothing. So there never was a Big Bang that created something from nothing.[52]

So the Big Bang didn't create something from nothing. Or did it?

Hawking then gave his thoughts about the actual beginning:

There must have been a beginning. Otherwise, the universe would be in a state of complete disorder by now...

Hawking brought it down to a level we can understand. The Second Law of Thermodynamics tells us that everything is running down. If the universe were eternal, it would have turned to dust trillions of years ago. There must, therefore, have been a beginning.

Here are more quotes from Professor Hawking:

- "We are just an advanced breed of monkeys on a minor planet of a very average star. But we can understand the universe. That makes us something very special."

- "For millions of years, mankind lived just like the animals. Then something happened which unleashed the power of our imagination. We learned to talk and we learned to listen. Speech has allowed the communication of ideas, enabling human beings to work together to build the impossible. Mankind's greatest achievements have come about by talking, and its greatest failures by not talking. It doesn't have to be like this. Our greatest hopes could become reality in the future. With the technology at our disposal, the possibilities are unbounded. All we need to do is make sure we keep talking."

- "My goal is simple. It is a complete understanding of the universe, why it is as it is and why it exists at all."

- "I believe the simplest explanation is, there is no God. No one created the universe and no one directs our fate. This leads me to a profound realization that there probably is no heaven and no afterlife either. We have this one life to appreciate the grand design of the universe and for that, I am extremely grateful."

It's also what the Bible says: "In the beginning God created the heavens and the earth" (Genesis 1:1). There's the beginning. Again, the Bible is the Instruction Book for humanity. It tells us of our origin, our purpose, and our destiny. We need not latch on to everything the gardener says. Instead, we need only believe the Word of the God who brought everything into existence. We will then know the truth, and the truth will make us free from endless and senseless theories.

But there's more. According to the gardener, nothing was there before the Big Bang. Nothing was the cause. There was, according to Hawking, no need for a Creator. All that was there was nothing, and that nothing created everything—flowers, birds, trees, kittens, giraffes, puppies, horses (all with male and female), as well as the blue sky, the sun, the moon, the stars, the four seasons, little green apples, and of course, simple gardeners.

The reporter who said, "Let Stephen Hawking blow your mind," then stated, "Hawking went on to basically explain that before the Big Bang, time didn't exist. So, yep! Mind sufficiently blown."[53]

The world's prophet has spoken. We don't dare question it.

FISHING WITH SAM

One cool morning in Southern California I set out on my bike as usual, looking for people with whom I could share the gospel. As I looked into the distance I saw a lone figure shooting hoops on a basketball court in a local park. As I rode toward him, he stopped and walked toward his duffel bag.

Here is how the conversation went: "Hey, what are you doing? Shooting hoops all by yourself?" He said he was, and I added, "This is Sam. Do you like dogs?" When he said he did, he stepped forward and patted Sam on the head.

I asked, "What's your name?"

"Barry."

"I'm Ray, Barry. I've got a question for you. Do you think there's an afterlife?"

He said he hoped there was, but he wasn't sure. Asked if he would go to Heaven when he died—was he a good person?—he said he was. When I asked him to estimate how many lies he had told in his life, he said he had lost count. He had stolen, and he had use God's name in vain a couple of times, but immediately apologized to God. When I began, "Jesus said...," he butted in and stated, "I'm Jewish." I responded, "So am I. Jesus said, 'Whoever looks at a woman to lust for her has already committed adultery with her in his heart.' Have you ever done that?" He had. Many times.

"Barry, I'm not judging you, but you have just told me that you are a lying, thieving, blasphemous adulterer at heart. If God judges you by the Ten Commandments—the Law of Moses that He gave to him on Mount Sinai—would you be innocent or guilty?"

"Guilty."

"Would you go to Heaven or Hell?"

Barry looked intently at me and said, "Jews don't believe in Hell. If you were Jewish, you would know that." I told him that the book of Psalms warns that all nations that forget God will be turned into Hell (Psalm 9:17), and that the Old Testament speaks of God's wrath (Deuteronomy 30:22; Psalm 2:12; 18:7; Isaiah 2:12; 14:15; Ezekiel 13:5; Daniel 12:2; Joel 1:15). I asked, "What do you think God should do with Hitler? Should he go to Heaven? Did the lives of six million Jews mean nothing to God? Of course, there must be a Day of Retribution. Of course, there must be a place called 'Hell' if God is just and holy and cares about right and wrong." Barry began nodding his head in agreement.

Then I told him that God did something wonderful for sinners so that we didn't have to go to Hell. He provided a Lamb. When John the Baptist saw Jesus walking toward him, he said, "Behold! The Lamb of God who takes away the sin of the world!" (John 1:29).

"Are you talking about the Passover?"

"Yes. Just as God provided a lamb for Abraham and Isaac, He provided a perfect sinless Lamb to suffer and die for the sin of the world." Then I explained the gospel more fully to Barry—how God had destroyed death, and of his need to repent and trust the Savior. Then I thanked him for listening to me, offered him a free movie card, and our coin with the Ten Commandments on one side and the gospel on the other. To my delight he took both gifts. We shook hands, and I thanked him for listening to me.

MORE FISHING

As I was riding down a pathway among some trees, I looked ahead and saw a tall woman walking in front of me. I decided that I would feel a little uncomfortable approaching the woman in case she thought I was trying to pick her up. But I stopped beside her anyway, and gave her a Ten Commandments coin. Then

I asked if she thought God existed. As I did so, I noticed that "she" had some tattoos and that her voice was that of a male. He said that his name was Summer, and he didn't want to talk about the things of God. I pleaded with him to just stay for a few moments. Thankfully, he did. I asked him if he was a good person. He said that he was. Then we went through the Ten Commandments without touching on the subject of homosexuality. We went to the cross and the necessity of repentance and faith.

He said he didn't want to live forever and he didn't love his life. When I asked if he'd ever had suicidal thoughts, he said that he did and that he had constant depression, which he said was caused by his father.

He then said he didn't believe in my God. I told him that was "idolatry," and I was guilty of it myself before I was a Christian. I had made up a god to suit myself—a snuggly teddy bear that I felt comfortable with, because there was no mention of justice, righteousness, or truth from my idol.

At that, he said he'd had enough and wanted to go. But when I asked if I could walk with him, he gave me permission.

Summer was a welder. He loved his job and had been doing it for ten years. For the next ten minutes I poured my heart and soul out to him, pleading with him to take seriously what we were talking about. Then I shared 1 Corinthians 6:9,10, about how adulterers, fornicators, and homosexuals would not inherit the kingdom of God.

When I asked him if he could detect an earnest sincerity in my tone, he said he could. I told him that I *really* cared about him and where he spent eternity. He took a Subway gift card, one of our movie gift cards, and promised he would think about what I had said. That was all I was asking. When I got back home, I spent some time in prayer for this lost soul.

QUESTIONS TO CONSIDER

1. What Bible verse inspired Matthew Maury to search for the paths of the sea?
2. Explain the science of oceanography.
3. What was Matthew Maury's "rule"?
4. How many gallons of water are estimated to make up the oceans?
5. How much water is locked up in ice caps and glaciers?
6. Explain the Second Law of Thermodynamics.
7. Would you feel nervous about mentioning Jesus to a Jew? If so, why?

6

THE HYDROLOGIC CYCLE

Weather is something we have every day whether we want it or not. In most parts of the world, it is the basis for beginning a conversation. "Good morning! Good afternoon! Nice day! Good to see the sun out," etc., are warm ice-breakers between strangers.

But weather is more than just a nice blue sky. It is defined as:

> ...the condition of the environment at any time—such as the temperature, cloud cover, fog conditions, air pressure, humidity and precipitation. Today the weather might be sunny with a clear sky and tomorrow there might be clouds and rain.[54]

It is sunshine—the rays of an exploding star 93 million miles away; rain—which is vast amounts of water weighing trillions of tons suspended in massive containers miles above us; and invisible winds swirling around the earth. While all this may sometimes seem chaotic, it's wonderfully ordered.

Most of us give little thought to the hydrologic cycle, as we give little thought to the functions of our body's vital organs. Human beings have five vital organs that are essential for our survival: the brain, heart, kidneys, liver, and lungs. Our brain is the body's control center. It sends and receives signals from other organs through the nervous system and through secreted hormones.

We also give little thought to the amazing cycle that governs the vital functions of water and air. What we normally call "weather" is a wonder of nature called the "hydrologic cycle," which was created by the genius of God. Of course, modern man thinks he now understands how weather works. Around 2,800 years ago, when it was believed that land floated on a body of water, and that most of the water in the rivers had their origin under the earth, the Bible spoke of the hydrologic cycle. Here's what we know now:

> The hydrologic cycle involves water moving from the surface (most importantly the oceans) to the atmosphere, across the land, and everywhere in between. Environmental scientists know that the hydrologic cycle includes various processes that change water from solid to liquid to gas form and transport it to every corner of earth's surface (and below). In terms of water, the earth is a closed system, so water isn't added or removed from earth; it's simply transformed, transported, and recycled.[55]

Examples of the hydrologic cycle in action can be seen in rivers:

> Another way to measure the size of a river is by the amount of water it discharges. Using this measure the Mississippi River is the 15th largest river in the world discharging 16,792 cubic meters (593,003 cubic feet) of water per second into the Gulf of Mexico. The biggest river by discharge volume is the Amazon at an impressive 209,000 cubic meters (7,380,765 cubic feet) per second. The Amazon drains a rainforest while the Mississippi drains much of the area between the Appalachian and Rocky Mountains, much of which is fairly dry.[56]

Where does all that water go? These are just two of thousands of rivers. The answer lies in the hydrologic cycle—something not fully understood until the seventeenth century, but so well brought out in the Bible.

Rivers pour into the ocean. Ocean water evaporates into the sky, and the clouds then pour water back onto the earth. The Scriptures say,

> He . . . calls for the waters of the sea, and pours them out on the face of the earth . . . (Amos 9:6)

> All the rivers run into the sea, yet the sea is not full; to the place from which the rivers come, there they return again. (Ecclesiastes 1:7)

> If the clouds are full of rain, they empty themselves upon the earth. (Ecclesiastes 11:7)

THE OFFICE PARTY

You're at an office party on the tenth floor of a high-rise, when you hear the distant sound of sirens. Everyone rushes to one of the windows to see what's happening. They are looking at another high-rise about eight feet from your building across a narrow alley.

Smoke is billowing from a window and you can see that a number of people are trapped! You hear gasps from those around you as they come to grips with the reality that within minutes, they are going to see people burned alive in front of their eyes. Suddenly of one your fellow workers turns and runs out of the office in a seeming panic. You wonder why he would be so cowardly as to run away.

Seconds later, he comes crashing through the door like a madman, across the office, and smashes the window with the front of a ten-foot ladder. The group then helps him to secure the ladder into the window of the opposing building. It is then that you see the wisdom of what he was doing as those trapped people begin, one by one, to crawl across the ladder to safety.

What was it that caused people to crawl across the ladder to safety? It was fear! It was the knowledge they had of what would happen to them if they stayed in the building.

Think now what the ladder would have meant to them if they didn't know that their own building was on fire. If they thought they were safe, someone in another building pushing a ladder across to their building would be more than meaningless. It would be reckless harassment, worthy of a call to the police.

We are looking at some of the scientific facts in the Bible. These facts are evidences that the Bible must be supernatural in origin. Having one or two scientific facts within its many pages could be written off as coincidental. But with ten scientific facts, a reasonable person must conclude that this Book is unique and therefore worthy of their attention. This is all we ask from the world. We are really saying, "Please listen! Your building is on fire!" The scientific facts are simply an attention-getter, but they don't show the world the danger. They are a distant alarm. What they really need is to smell the smoke and think of their fate.

The whole sinful world is in a burning building. Sin is seen as a pleasurable party rather than a danger. The gospel is foolishness to them, and our pleading with them is nothing but harassment. We talk of everlasting life being a free gift of God, and they accuse us of pushing religion down their throats.

Their rejection of the best news they could ever hope to hear is unbelievable. Unbelievable that is, until you understand what is happening. They love their sin. And what's more, God doesn't seem to be bothered by it. It's no big deal. Lying, stealing, lust, blasphemy, fornication, and even adultery don't bring the slightest lightning strike from Heaven. A haunting feeling of guilt, yes, but no wrath from God—thus there's no danger. And the voice of an unruly conscience can easily be quieted. Ecclesiastes 8:11 says,

> Because the sentence against an evil work is not executed speedily, therefore the heart of the sons of men is fully set in them to do evil.

God's mercy holds back His wrath. He is not willing that any should perish, and so He waits patiently waits for them to repent:

But, beloved, do not forget this one thing, that with the Lord one day is as a thousand years, and a thousand years as one day. The Lord is not slack concerning His promise, as some count slackness, but is longsuffering toward us, not willing that any should perish but that all should come to repentance. But the day of the Lord will come as a thief in the night, in which the heavens will pass away with a great noise, and the elements will melt with fervent heat; both the earth and the works that are in it will be burned up. (2 Peter 3:8–10)

The world is in terrible danger! They *must* be warned, and God has given us the moral Law to help them to smell the smoke and see their danger. When we open up the Commandments, the sinner whose conscience is awakened by the Holy Spirit will smell the smoke of the wrath of God. Those who do suddenly see that we love them, and that the ladder of the gospel of Christ is their only means of salvation.

FISHING WITH SAM

It was 7 a.m. on Saturday morning. I could see, about fifty yards in front of me, a man sitting on a bench by the sidewalk and thought of a number of reasons why I shouldn't stop and witness to him. The first was that it was way too early in the morning to talk about the things of God. The second reason was that it was probably the same gentleman who was sitting there a week earlier who coldly rejected my offer of a Ten Commandments coin.

So I rode past him and wished him a good morning. As I did so, his response was extremely warm. *It was not the same man.* I stopped my bike, backed up and handed him a coin, saying, "Did I give you one of these? It's a coin with the Ten Commandments on one side and the gospel on the other."

When he thanked me, I asked if he was a Christian. He said he was a Catholic. When I asked if he had been born again, he smiled and said, "I've only been born once." I told him that Jesus (in John chapter 3) said that if we haven't been born again we're not going to Heaven. "It's like the difference between *believing* in a parachute and actually *putting one on*. You'll see your mistake the moment you jump."

He smiled and said, "Good analogy." When I asked Joe if he thought he was a good person, he said he was. After we'd been through the Commandments he said he thought that his good outweighed his bad. I explained to him why that won't even work in a court of law, let alone on Judgment Day.

"If a criminal says, 'Judge, I robbed the bank, but I give money to the Red Cross,' the judge is going to say that his good deeds have *nothing* to do with his crimes. He will be judged only on the crimes he committed. Then I explained the cross, and added once again to put his faith in Christ and not in himself and in his good works.

"If you ever jump out of a plane, don't try to save yourself by flapping your arms. Trust in the parachute alone to save you. Don't trust in your good works because you don't have any in God's eyes. Trust alone in Christ."

I then gave him a gift card and thanked him for listening. Joe seemed pleased that I had stopped and spoken to him. Once again, so was I.

QUESTIONS TO CONSIDER

1. Define "weather."
2. What did people believe about the earth 2,800 years ago?
3. Explain the hydrologic cycle.
4. Identify some of the verses in the Bible that speak of the hydrologic cycle.
5. What role can scientific facts play in our evangelism efforts?
6. What analogy could you use to explain why "good works" will never save us?
7. What has God given us to help awaken the world to its danger?

THE FIRST LAW OF THERMODYNAMICS

Samuel Butler said, "Life is one long process of getting tired." Children don't seem to get tired. They are filled with an energy that exhausts most parents. As much as we try to conserve youthful vitality, time takes it from us. As we age, what energy we do have dissipates and finally . . . it runs out, and we die.

And yet the First Law of Thermodynamics (also referred to as the Law of the Conservation of Energy and/or Mass) states that neither matter nor energy can be either created or destroyed. One way to understand this is to realize that there is no "creation" ongoing today. It is "finished" exactly as the Bible states:

> Thus the heavens and the earth, and all the host of them, were finished. (Genesis 2:1)

Everything is finished. Nature is complete. The brilliance of the light-giving sun is complete. It doesn't need to be bigger, smaller, hotter, or cooler. Neither does it need to be closer or more distant. It is perfectly constructed and positioned for what it does for us. The heavens are finished. The clouds do what they are designed to do. They drop the rain, cleansing the air and giving life to the earth. Tall trees are finished, giving us oxygen to breathe. The rivers are finished as they meander across the face of the earth, filling our great oceans with water through the finished hydroelectric cycle. The waters are teaming with finished fish—with their finished gills, scales, and tails, and the soil making up the land is finished, yielding plants from seeds to give us food to eat. Peaches, pears, pineapples, plums, papayas, pumpkins, and peas are all finished. Nothing is incomplete.

Study your hand for a moment. Unless you have some sort of abnormality or you've had an accident, the hand is functionally perfect. It bends forward for gripping. The complex muscles under the skin align themselves for forward movement. The nails are curved and the finger skin is strong but sensitive. If you lose a hand, experts imitate its design when creating a prosthesis, but they *can't* improve on its finished design. The four fingers and one thumb are perfect for gripping. If you were designing a man-made replacement for a human hand, what improvements would you suggest? Three fingers? Two thumbs? Bending backwards? Would you have the body produce three hands? We can't improve on God's finished and wonderful design.

Nothing in nature has a half-evolved eye, ear, leg, or brain. It's *all* finished, from the animals, to man, to wings of birds, to butterflies, to the beauty and fragrance of the rose that blossoms to God's glory and for our pleasure. Nothing is evolving, everything is finished just as the Bible said 3,000 years ago.

Think further with your finished and functioning brain about the finished state of the human body. Fallen though it is, it is a marvel of completed design. Hair grows from the scalp. We don't think deeply about how amazing the condition of the scalp is, until hair begins to drop out. Think of how hair grows in different directions. Think of what makes it grow, and how it's different from eyebrow hair, or the eyelashes, or wiry beard-hair. Eyelashes stop at a certain point but neither scalp hair nor beard hair know when to stop. Despite that, hair is finished. It is completed as hair. It's functional and cosmetic.

Teeth are also finished. You get two sets, and you get two rows. Each of the functionally designed teeth grew from your jaw into a particular purposeful shape. Front teeth are cutting-edge. They have been designed for cutting and the back teeth for chewing. They are finished. Your front teeth don't keep growing. They are done. Ready for action.

So is your skin finished. It's perfectly holding everything in. It doesn't keep growing. Stretching, yes, if you overeat. But it is complete in its purpose. It's the same with your wonderfully made eyes. You're not going to evolve another cyclops eye between your existing eyes. They are *perfectly* coordinated. You can see. They're done. The same applies with your ears, arms, heart, liver, lungs, and those more private parts. Everything is finished. It's fully functional. Ready for action. Done. Just as the Bible says.

THE AGE OF THE EARTH AND UNIVERSE

One great stumbling block for many is the issue of the age of the universe. According to Space.com:

> Age may only be a number, but when it comes to the age of the universe, it's a pretty important one. According to research, the universe is approximately 13.8 billion years old. How did scientists determine how many candles to put on the universe's birthday cake? They can determine the age of the universe using two different methods: by studying the oldest objects within the universe and measuring how fast it is expanding.
>
> The universe cannot be younger than the objects contained inside of it. By determining the ages of the oldest stars, scientists are able to put a limit on the age.
>
> The life cycle of a star is based on its mass. More massive stars burn faster than their lower-mass siblings. A star 10 times as massive as the sun will burn through its fuel supply in 20 million years, while a star with half the sun's mass will last more than 20 billion years. The mass also affects the brightness, or luminosity, of a star; more massive stars are brighter.[57]

But here's the problem. They are not accounting for the fact that everything God created was finished. If a scientist used the same process for aging newly created Adam, even though he was brand new off the assembly line, they would be certain he was about thirty years old. And they would be wrong.

UNFINISHED BUSINESS

Yet in all of this finished creation, God has given us the ability to start new things. We can make cakes, cars, clothes, casseroles, and cats. We can interbreed animals and create new breeds, just like we often create new words.

For example, have you ever heard of the word "compofluous"? I'm sure it's a new word to many people. It means "something that seems ridiculous, and yet is a reality." We take it for granted that massive planes weighing hundreds of tons can fly across the sky. Two hundred years ago such a thought would have been ridiculous. But planes are a reality. The fact that we can see and talk to people on the other side of the world, at the speed of light—without the use of wires—would have seemed absurd one hundred years ago. But things like Skype and FaceTime are facts of life. Much of what we call "modern technology" is compofluous.

It was because I kept misspelling the word "Thanks" as "Thnaks" at the end of emails that I considered making it a new word. That would have solved my typo problem. That thought sparked the question as to who it is that makes up new words. Could "Thnaks" ever be seriously considered as an alternative word to express appreciation?

After some research, I discovered that it is *dictionary publishers* who determine what to add to the million or so existing English words, and that they come up with about a thousand new words each year.

The Guardian reported,

But these represent just a sliver of the tip of the iceberg. According to Global Language Monitor, around 5,400 new words are created every year; it's only the 1,000 or so deemed to be in sufficiently widespread use that make it into print.[58]

So in a sense, it's not even the dictionary dudes who dictate whether or not a new word lives, but its popularity.

Another curiosity I have has to do with the first word that Adam said. I wonder what it was? "Hello"? "Huh"? "Hey"? Or as a brand-new human being, was he like a newborn babe in his understanding? I doubt that he began life with "Goo-goo" and "Dadda." Or even "Duh." I think God would have given him the intuitive ability to think, speak, communicate. He would have been mature in body, mind, and soul—finished, like everything else. That meant that he had the ability to speak a complete and intelligible language. Here are his first recorded words given to us in Scripture:

> And the Lord God caused a deep sleep to fall on Adam, and he slept; and He took one of his ribs, and closed up the flesh in its place. Then the rib which the Lord God had taken from man He made into a woman, and He brought her to the man. And Adam said:

> "This is now bone of my bones
> And flesh of my flesh;
> She shall be called Woman,
> Because she was taken out of Man." (Genesis 2:21–23)

He was discerning, intelligent, educated, and had the ability to reason and exercise initiative. Adam made up a new word: "Woman." Previous to this, he'd been busy making up other new words for the Eden dictionary—words for animals that presumably had huge ears, long trunks, extended necks, massive tails, stripes or patches, that mooed, barked, and squawked—animals that crawled, jumped, walked, flew, and ran. God brought them to him specifically to be named by Adam:

> Out of the ground the Lord God formed every beast of the field and every bird of the air, and brought them to Adam to see what he would call them. And whatever Adam called each living creature, that was its name. So Adam gave names to all cattle, to the birds of the air, and to every beast of the field. But for Adam there was not found a helper comparable to him. (Genesis 2:19,20)

Necessity is the mother of invention, and the fact that Adam was surrounded by so many animals meant that he needed help. It wasn't good that man should be alone (Genesis 2:18); he needed a companion, a life mate. But this new creation didn't come from the soil; there was nothing dirty about it. Neither was it an animal. The woman was, like Adam, made in the image of God— a special creation, which came as a special delivery. God Himself presented this present to him. It was different from the massive elephants, the tall giraffes, or the beautiful birds. It walked upright on two legs like him. It was made of the same flesh as Adam, but had a different shape and look. Mind-bogglingly attractive and different.

Eye has not seen nor ear heard, nor could it enter into our imaginations what it was like in that garden, because our imaginations are based on what we know of this fallen world. Eden must have been out of this world.

MINOR MIRACLES

It would have been strange for Adam to have audibly expressed himself from the moment of his creation, especially if he did it with no knowledge of the origin of his words. But even in our fallen state, we see minor miracles. How is it that a baby looks into the eyes of his parents? No one teaches him to do that. So many things happen in life that don't make sense. How is it that a small child uses the word "actually"? It's common to hear it. Most adults would hesitate to be able to explain the right use of the word if we were put on the spot. Yet a small child uses it in the correct context, without any definitive training.

But think of a man who has severe amnesia. He actually doesn't remember anything—who he is or where he is from. As far as he is concerned, he didn't exist until the moment he awoke from a coma. Yet he can actually express himself, and if he was educated, he does so with eloquent words. Actually, it does seem ridiculous that any man would have no knowledge that he could speak, and yet to his own amazement, he can speak and do so eloquently. Which is certainly compofluous—"something that seems ridiculous, and yet is a reality." Actually, I made up the word, and would be grateful if you would try to use it daily—which may seem ridiculous, but if enough people use it, it may become a reality, and that would be compofluous.

FISHING WITH SAM

I hope you don't get the impression that every time I witness to someone it goes wonderfully well. I have already overused "actually," so I won't use it now even though it would fit. But I had four bad witnessing sessions in a row recently.

The first occurred when I was riding my bike past a gentleman, who was perhaps in his early seventies, who responded to my greeting in a friendly manner. I had gone about three hundred yards past him when I decided that if I *really* cared about him I would go back and share the gospel. So I rode all the way back and said, "Did I give you one of these?" As he took the Ten Commandments coin, I said, "It's the Ten Commandments with the gospel on the other side." He held his hand out and said, "I'd like to give this back to you." I replied, "It's yours. If you don't want it, feel free to throw it away."

Suddenly the man began a tirade against Christians in America, saying that 98 percent were hypocrites. I said that God would judge them if they were hypocrites, and asked him about the 2 percent who were genuine. He was very angry, was pro-abortion, and was for everything that Christians are against. We talked for about ten minutes, during which time I was able to share the gospel. But he couldn't take any more, turned around, and walked away with great clouds of smoke billowing from his ears.

He was a hate-filled and prejudicial man, who said that Christians will go to Hell. I didn't have a warm and fuzzy feeling as I rode away. But I did thank God that I was able to share the gospel with him, even if it was rather quick. At least the man listened as I did so.

The next day, I stopped at the local skateboard park and found to my surprise that the skateboarder I had seen from a distance was a female in her early twenties. I felt awkward as I tried to break the ice with small-talk. I said that I wasn't trying to pick her up to which she wisely said that she didn't want to talk to a stranger. I responded that I was a Christian, and that I just wanted to share the gospel. The ice didn't break. It was now *really* awkward, so I moved on—about four hundred yards down the bike path, and stopped near a man whose name was Glenn.

Glenn's fingers were covered with nicotine stains. He smoked a cigarette as we talked for a few moments about how much he received each month from the government as a retired beneficiary. Then I asked, "Glenn, do you think there is an afterlife?" He thought there definitely was, and that he was going to Heaven. If fact, *everybody* was going there. When I asked if Adolf Hitler was therefore going to make it, he said it wasn't his place to judge. He said he was a good person, adding that he blasphemed all the time, lied, and stole, and continually lusted for women. Then he said that he had "Christ," and didn't need someone persecuting him and going on about Hitler. And he didn't want to hear any more. Even when I said, "Thank you, sir, for listening to me," he stayed angry and walked off in the other direction.

There's more...

It was before 8:00 a.m. on a Saturday morning a few weeks later, when I saw an elderly man walking intently ahead of us (Sam and I). As I passed him, I wished him a warm good morning, but his response was even more enthusiastic, so I stopped, grabbed a coin and said, "Did I give you one of these?" His reply was to ask what I was selling. I said, "Nothing. It's a coin with the

Ten Commandments on one side and the gospel on the other." He looked at me with disgust and tried to give it back. I said, "It's yours, sir." He then tossed it down and said, "I don't need it!" I said, "Yes, you do, sir." When he walked away, I said, "Nice to meet you, sir. I hope you have a good day." He didn't reply.

I never get used to rejection, and when it comes, it tries to sit on me like a heavy cloud, stealing my joy. But I have learned not to let what may seem like a negative reaction discourage me. God only knows why the man acted that way. And He only knows if he became haunted by the words, "Yes, you do, sir." I prayed that was the case.

There were four witnessing sessions in a row that weren't "successful." But God doesn't require what we think of as success. He wants *faithfulness* from us, and He handles the rest.

One more...

It was 8:30 on the same morning that I rode past a woman who was smoking a cigarette on the steps of our ministry. She had a child with her, probably about two years old—which normally isn't the best scenario for sharing the gospel (kids tend to distract a parent). However, I stopped and did my usual routine, offering her the coin, going through the Commandments into the gospel, and then giving her the card and a free book I had written on the subject of depression and suicide.

She was really taken aback that I had stopped and spoken to her, and thanked me a number of times. As I was riding away she called out, "Thank you so much for taking the time to stop and talk to me."

Never let a negative experience hold you back from sharing the gospel. Just keep on sharing, and it's only a matter of time until the cloud dissipates and the sun comes shining through.

QUESTIONS TO CONSIDER

1. Explain the First Law of Thermodynamics.
2. Where does the Bible say that everything was "finished"?
3. Give some examples of things being finished in nature.
4. Give some examples of things being finished in the human body.
5. How long ago did the Bible mention the First Law of Thermodynamics?
6. What is the meaning of "compofluous"?
7. What does God require of us?

8

SHIP DIMENSIONS

In Genesis 6:15, God gave Noah the dimensions of the 1.88 million cubic foot ark he was to build. According to Answers in Genesis, Ken Ham's ministry:

> Noah's Ark was the focus of a major 1993 scientific study headed by Dr. Seon Hong at the world-class ship research center KRISO, based in Daejeon, South Korea. Dr. Hong's team compared twelve hulls of different proportions to discover which design was most practical. No hull shape was found to significantly outperform the 4,300-year-old biblical design. In fact, the Ark's careful balance is easily lost if the proportions are modified, rendering the vessel either unstable, prone to fracture, or dangerously uncomfortable.

The research team found that the proportions of Noah's Ark carefully balanced the conflicting demands of stability (resistance to capsizing), comfort ("seakeeping"), and strength. In fact, the Ark has the same proportions as a modern cargo ship.

The study also confirmed that the Ark could handle waves as high as 100 ft (30 m). Dr. Hong is now director general of the facility and claims "life came from the sea," obviously not the words of a creationist on a mission to promote the worldwide Flood. Endorsing the seaworthiness of Noah's Ark obviously did not damage Dr. Hong's credibility.[59]

Many contemporary ships are built with similar proportions, although the length-to-breadth ratio is usually chosen with regard to the power required to move them through the water. The ark needed only to keep afloat.

Scientists at the University of Leicester have discovered that Noah's Ark could have carried 70,000 animals without sinking if built from the dimensions listed in the Bible.

Noah's Ark would have floated even with two of every animal in the world packed inside, scientists have calculated. Although researchers are unsure if all the creatures could have squeezed into the huge boat, they are confident it would have handled the weight of 70,000 creatures without sinking.[60]

Here now is an intellectual dilemma for the proud skeptic. If the evidence for the ark is at all compelling, he should be prepared to go where it leads. But this evidence is going to lead him down Humiliation Street. Surely, he thinks, the Noah's Ark story is a myth. It's in the same category as "Little Red Riding Hood" and "Jack and the Beanstalk." These stories may have some redeeming message—some sort of life-lesson—but they should never be taken literally. There was no talking wolf, or giant in the sky, and

Noah didn't build an ark and float two of every creature in it. To say you actually believe in a talking wolf, or that a giant really did live in the sky at the top of a massive beanstalk, would make you the butt of jokes, even to the grandchildren to whom you read the story.

It takes humility to follow this evidence, and humility and faith in Jesus is the only highway to Heaven. We looked earlier at how a famous atheist, Antony Flew, changed his mind about the existence of God, because he had the humility to follow the evidence to where it led him. He explained in an interview:

> There were two factors in particular that were decisive. One was my growing empathy with the insight of Einstein and other noted scientists that there had to be an Intelligence behind the integrated complexity of the physical Universe. The second was my own insight that the integrated complexity of life itself—which is far more complex than the physical Universe—can only be explained in terms of an Intelligent Source. I believe that the origin of life and reproduction simply cannot be explained from a biological standpoint despite numerous efforts to do so. With every passing year, the more that was discovered about the richness and inherent intelligence of life, the less it seemed likely that a chemical soup could magically generate the genetic code. The difference between life and non-life, it became apparent to me, was ontological and not chemical. The best confirmation of this radical gulf is Richard Dawkins' comical effort to argue in *The God Delusion* that the origin of life can be attributed to a "lucky chance." If that's the best argument

you have, then the game is over. No, I did not hear a Voice. It was the evidence itself that led me to this conclusion.[61]

FISHING WITHOUT SAM

Here is a huge key to conquering the Goliath of fear. Have a plan that you begin putting into action. I was on my way home without Sam when I saw a gentleman and a dog about one hundred yards in front of me. *I had a plan.* I was going to speak to him. So I put that plan into action. I committed myself by grabbing a Ten Commandments coin and holding it in my hand.

As I approach the gentleman, I asked, "Did I give you one of these?" That question stirs curiosity and makes the person feel that they are missing out on something. Which they are, if they don't take it. He replied, "One of what?" That's when I handed it to him and said, "It's a coin with the Ten Commandments on it, and the gospel on the other side." I then asked, "Do you think there's an afterlife?"

He hesitatingly said that he did and added, "All you have to do is keep the Ten Commandments, and you will be okay." That was my cue.

Edmond turned out to be a lying, thieving, blasphemous adulterer at heart—someone who had violated four of the Commandments, would be guilty on Judgment Day, and would end up in Hell. His body language was similar to that of an Olympic runner waiting at the starting line. He wanted to get out of there quickly.

I said, "I can see that you want to leave, so I'll be quick." I shared the gospel with him telling him that at the moment he was like a man who was flapping his arms when he jumped out of a plane at 10,000 feet. I encouraged him to trust in Jesus alone, thanked him for listening to me, and asked if I could give him a gift. When I offered him a gift card, his demeanor radically changed. His facial expression then looked like he had just won an Olympic race. It was good to see.

QUESTIONS TO CONSIDER

1. Where in Scripture did God give Noah the dimensions of the ark?
2. What would have been Noah's message to the world?
3. What is our message?
4. What are some biblical facts about the ark that modern scientists have corroborated?
5. Why do so many in the world stumble at the biblical story of Noah's ark?
6. Name some of the evidences that led Antony Flew to logically conclude there is an Intelligent Designer.
7. What is a key to conquering our fear of witnessing?

9

LAWS OF QUARANTINE

In the book of Leviticus, the Bible speaks of quarantine, long before medical science discovered the importance of isolating those who had infectious diseases. In 1490 BC, the Bible gave instructions on what to do with those who have a skin condition like leprosy:

> All the days he has the sore he shall be unclean. He is unclean, and he shall dwell alone; his dwelling shall be outside the camp. (Leviticus 13:46)

Laws of quarantine were not instigated by modern man until the seventeenth century. The devastating Black Death of the fourteenth century took an estimated 70 million lives. This is because they failed to separate the sick from the healthy. When whole families fell ill, it was attributed to bad air. However, putting into practice the ordinances of quarantine laid out in Scripture would have saved millions of lives.

HISTORY OF QUARANTINE

NOVA, a secular source, acknowledged that the history of quarantine included its roots in Scripture:

> The practice of quarantine—the separation of the diseased from the healthy—has been around a long time. As early as the writing of the Old Testament, for instance, rules existed for isolating lepers...In the mid-20th century, the advent of antibiotics and routine vaccinations made large-scale quarantines a thing of the past, but today bioterrorism and newly emergent diseases like SARS threaten to resurrect the age-old custom, potentially on the scale of entire cities.[62]

According to the Centers for Disease Control and Prevention (CDC), quarantine was started in the fourteenth century. Either they are ignorant of Scripture or they don't give any credence to the Bible:

> The practice of quarantine, as we know it, began during the 14th century in an effort to protect coastal cities from plague epidemics. Ships arriving in Venice from infected ports were required to sit at anchor for 40 days before landing. This practice, called quarantine, was derived from the Italian words *quaranta giorni* which mean 40 days.[63]

It would seem that no one knows where the forty-day period of quarantine originated. This is from an article on Oxford Academic:

> The precise rationale for changing the isolation period from 30 days to 40 days is not known. Some authors sug-

gest that it was changed because the shorter period was insufficient to prevent disease spread. Others believe that the change was related to the Christian observance of Lent, a 40-day period of spiritual purification. Still others believe that the 40-day period was adopted to reflect the duration of other biblical events, such as the great flood, Moses' stay on Mt. Sinai, or Jesus' stay in the wilderness. Perhaps the imposition of 40 days of isolation was derived from the ancient Greek doctrine of "critical days," which held that contagious disease will develop within 40 days after exposure. Although the underlying rationale for changing the duration of isolation may never be known, the fundamental concept embodied in the *quarantino* has survived and is the basis for the modern practice of quarantine.[64]

THE ISOLATION OF THE LEPER

In Jude 1:22,23 we are told, "And on some have compassion, making a distinction; but others save with fear, pulling them out of the fire, hating even the garment defiled by the flesh." Bible commentator Matthew Poole said of these New Testament verses:

Hating even the garment spotted by the flesh: it is an allusion to that ceremonial law, Leviticus 15:4,17, where he that touched a defiled garment was himself defiled. The sense is, either:

1. That where there is danger of infection from heretics and obstinate sinners, all converse with them, and any thing whereby the contagion of their doctrine or manners may reach us, is to be avoided: or:

2. That when we reprehend others, we should do it with suitable affections, and though we would save themselves, we should hate their vices, and any thing that promotes them or savors of them.[65]

Leprosy in the Old Testament is a type of sin. It's a disease that destroys the nerves and makes the sufferer incapable of feeling pain. To the uninformed this seems like a blessing, when in truth it's the opposite. Pain causes us to move and allow blood to flow. If you are seated, every now and then you will feel uncomfortable and change your position in your seat, otherwise you would go numb in the area. The same happens while you're asleep. You toss and turn, because if you comfortably stayed in one position, the blood couldn't flow through your flesh, and it would rot. That's what happens with leprosy. The flesh rots because the sufferer is not aware of the need to move.

Sin does the same thing. It dulls the nerves of the conscience. There is no moral discomfort when one lies or steals, blasphemes or fornicates. The desire to move away from evil disappears, and the sinner begins to morally rot. The consequence is that he will be isolated forever in a terrible place called Hell.

FISHING WITH SAM

My heart sank as I looked into the distance in front of me. I wanted to witness to the next person I saw, because I had so many rejections previously. One guy turned around and saw me and had mumbled, "Oh, no! Not you; go away." The next person had a dog that barked so incessantly neither of us could hear the other speak. The reason my heart sank was that the man in front of me also had a dog with him.

I stopped anyway and asked the name of the dog. Then I told the man I had a gift for him. After hearing that it contained the Ten Commandments, he tried to give it back to me. When I said, "No, it's yours," he said he might throw it away. His name was Rob, and he said his parents were Christians, his father was a pastor, and he wasn't interested in anything to do with religion. I suspected that Rob was a homosexual, but I wasn't sure. However, he was very nice and polite and allowed me to take him through the Commandments.

Whenever I witness to homosexuals, I stay with the Commandments and don't talk about their sexual life. In this way they can see they are in terrible eternal danger, *despite* their sexual preference. But as I got to the gospel Rob became very uncomfortable. So I said, "I've got another gift for you. It's a Subway gift card. I want you to know that I really do care about you."

With that, he seemed taken aback and allowed me to share the rest of the gospel. Then we talked about living in California. He said he appreciated that it was a state that believed in diversity, which confirmed my suspicions that he was homosexual. I told him again that I cared about him, and that his parents cared where he spent eternity. I then gave him a book called *How to Battle Depression and Suicidal Thoughts*. He become very congenial and seemed to be thankful that we had our talk. As with many times before, I certainly was.

SMOG CHECK

My car needed a smog check plus a couple of other repairs, so I had to leave it in the garage for about two hours. That meant I had to walk home.

While I was walking, I saw a rather shabby gentleman in his sixties, working in his garden. So I called, "How are you doing?" He replied, "Good. How are you?" I said great, and asked, "Are you reading your Bible?" He responded, "Not any more," adding that he had lost faith. When I asked him why that had happened, he said it was because of all the bad things that were going on in the world. I said, "You don't throw away your parachute just because the flight gets bumpy. You cling tighter to it."

He then put down his weed-eater and walked toward me. As he did so, I asked for his name. It was Tom.

When I asked him if he was a good person, he said, "Off and on." But after going through the Commandments he found that he was a lying, thieving, blasphemous adulterer at heart, and he was heading for Hell. Then I shared the gospel with him.

Tom was very likable but had a very dirty mouth, especially when I talked about God punishing the world with death. He told me he was a Roman Catholic and said he was happy with that. I wasn't, so I reasoned with him further about how we can't earn eternal life, that God won't be bribed, and about the character and nature of God, how He was holy and that on the Day of Judgment all He will do is carry out perfect justice. I told him that I loved him and was deeply concerned about where he would spend eternity. I gave him a gift card, which spoke volumes to him.

Tom's house was unique because there was a massive tree in the front yard that looked as though it was dead. But he said it wasn't, and it would come alive in the spring. I told him that tree was like his life. He was as good as dead, but if he would repent and trust Jesus, the life of God will spring forth in him. I encouraged him to think about that whenever he looked at the tree. When I asked if he had a Bible, he said that he had three or four. He asked for my name, reached out his hand and shook mine, saying that he would think about what we talked about.

QUESTIONS TO CONSIDER

1. Where does Scripture speak of quarantine?
2. When does the CDC believe quarantine began?
3. Discuss how you would feel if you had leprosy and were quarantined.
4. How is leprosy like sin?
5. What does Jude 1:22,23 say our attitude and actions should be?
6. When witnessing to homosexuals, is it necessary to talk about their sex life?
7. What are you doing to reach this world?

10

THE DINOSAUR

Many times I had heard skeptics say something like, "How come the Bible doesn't mention dinosaurs?" The inference is that the Bible is unscientific and archaic. They are saying, "It doesn't even mention these massive creatures of which we have proof. We have their bones. The Bible therefore isn't the Word of God, because it doesn't even mention them." Actually, it does.

In the following passage, God Himself speaks of a great creature called "behemoth":

> "Behold now, Behemoth, which I created as well as you; he eats grass like an ox. See now, his strength is in his loins and his power is in the muscles and sinews of his belly. He sways his tail like a cedar; the tendons of his thighs are twisted and knit together [like a rope]. His bones are tubes of bronze; his limbs are like bars of iron. He is the first [in magnitude and power] of the works of God..." (Job 40:15–19, AMP)

Allan Steel, writing in the *Journal of Creation*, explains:

The word "Behemoth" (Job 40:15) is literally a plural form of a common Old Testament (OT) word meaning "beast." However, practically all commentators and translators have agreed that here we have an intensive or majestic plural, so that the meaning is something like "colossal beast." This case is similar to the word "Elohim" (the most common name of God in the OT), which is actually a majestic plural form, but is always used with a singular verbal form, just as is encountered in this passage. Also, we read in verse 19 that Behemoth was the "chief of the ways of God," which suggests that Behemoth was one of the largest (if not the largest) of God's creatures.[66]

Some Bible commentators think this is a reference to the elephant or the hippopotamus. However, one of the characteristics of this massive animal is that it had a tail the size of a large tree. Neither the hippo nor the elephant fit this description. Both have only a twig of a tail.

Here, from Scripture, are the characteristics of this huge animal:

- It was the largest of all the creatures God made.
- It was plant-eating (herbivorous).
- It had its tremendous strength in its hips and belly.
- It had a tail like a large tree.
- It had very strong bones.
- It had limbs that were like bars of iron.

There are some who point out that the Bible could not be referring to a dinosaur in Job 40, as it uses the phrase (in the KJV) "his strength is in his loins, and his force is in the navel of his belly," and dinosaurs are all believed to have hatched from eggs, which negates that they had a navel.

(That brings up another point: which came first, the dinosaur or the egg? If it was the egg, it raises the question, was the egg fertilized? It must have been, or it wouldn't produce a dinosaur. How then did that happen? It must have been the product of a male and a female dinosaur, which brought forth after their own kind. That sounds remarkably like the biblical model of creation.)

The answer to the "navel of his belly" question can be found in the original Hebrew language. The original word translated in the King James version as "navel" is *shariyr*, which is defined in the Hebrew Lexicon by Heinrich Gesenius (often referred to as the father of modern Hebrew Lexicography) as being "the firm parts of the belly, i.e. the nerves, ligaments, muscles."[67] So it's simply a translation issue. A modern translation, such as the New King James version, words it as "his power is in his stomach muscles."

Therefore, there is only one creature that fits this description from the book of Job: the dinosaur.

National Geographic sheds a little more light on the Behemoth in an article entitled "Huge Dinosaur Footprints Discovered on Scottish Coast":

> The tracks shed light on dinosaur life in the Middle Jurassic, a period from which few fossils have survived...

> In a way, the discovery brings scientists' understanding of sauropods full circle. In the early 1900s, paleontologists

incorrectly viewed long-necked dinosaurs as lumbering brutes confined to swamps, their heavy bodies buoyed by water. Based on evidence gathered since then, it seems the behemoths did walk on terra firma, and they achieved global distribution. Sauropod bones and footprints have been found on all seven continents—including Antarctica.

"It wasn't that the water was the only place they could live and just had to languish," says [paleontologist Steve] Brusatte. "Instead, we're now saying that they were so dynamic and so energetic—that they were so successful—that they were probably exploring whatever environments they could."[68]

WHY DID THE DINOSAUR DISAPPEAR?

There are many theories about the dinosaurs' disappearance. Here's one reported in *Science Daily*:

The debate goes on: What killed off the dinosaurs?

New University of Oregon research has identified gravity-related fluctuations dating to 66 million years ago along deep ocean ridges that point to a "one-two punch" from the big meteor that struck off Mexico's Yucatan peninsula, possibly triggering a worldwide release of volcanic magma that could have helped seal the dinosaurs' fate. "We found evidence for a previously unknown period of globally heightened volcanic activity during the mass-extinction event," said former UO doctoral student Joseph Byrnes.[69]

Some have more than a theory; they think they *know*. The following article is titled "Here's What Happened the Day the Dinosaurs Died":

Imagine sunrise on the last day of the Mesozoic era, 66 million years ago . . . For a few fleeting moments, a fireball that appears far bigger and brighter than the sun streaks through the sky. An instant later, the asteroid slams into Earth with an explosive yield estimated at over 100 trillion tons of TNT.

The impact penetrates Earth's crust to a depth of several miles, gouging a crater more than 115 miles (185 kilometers) across and vaporizing thousands of cubic miles of rock. The event sets off a chain of global catastrophes that wipe out 80 percent of life on Earth—including most of the dinosaurs . . . But exactly how the fallout killed off so much life on Earth has remained a tantalizing mystery.[70]

A UC Berkeley website says,

Many hypotheses about dinosaur extinction sound quite convincing and might even be correct, but, as you know, are *not really science* if they cannot be proven or disproved. Even with the best hypothesis, such as the impact hypothesis, it is very difficult to prove or disprove whether the dinosaurs were rendered extinct by an event that occurred around the K-T boundary, or whether they were just weakened (or unaffected) by the event . . . Ultimately, a time machine would be required to see exactly what killed the dinosaurs.[71]

Answers in Genesis gives clear light on the subject:

Billions of animals were buried in the global Flood, but the Flood did not kill all the dinosaurs. God wanted animals preserved for a new start in the post-Flood world. When God told Noah to build an Ark to keep his family safe, He instructed Noah to take at least two of every kind of air-breathing, land-dwelling animal onto the Ark. Therefore, a pair of every dinosaur kind was on the Ark. At the end of the Flood, these dinosaurs disembarked. But the world was very different from the one they had left...

Dinosaurs faced the same sorts of challenges in the post-Flood world that endangered animals do today. In addition to adjusting to habitat changes, alterations in food availability, and competition from other animals, post-Flood dinosaur populations may have gradually succumbed to diseases or been hunted until their populations dwindled. So how did dinosaurs die? The same sorts of problems that drive today's animals to extinction took their toll on earth's remaining dinosaurs. But just as we don't need a cosmic culprit like a giant asteroid to explain the extinction of other animals, we don't need it to explain why we don't find dinosaurs in our zoos either.[72]

Then again, who says that the dinosaur disappeared? Darwinian evolution knows no such bounds. It's as big as the human imagination:

Are Birds Modern-Day Dinosaurs?

Modern birds consist of 247 families and 10,731 species, more than any other vertebrate group except fish. An asteroid strike 66 million years ago devastated the dinosaurs. But today's birds are proof there were a few survivors...

Birds are exceptionally diverse, with more than 10,000 known species—all of them the descendants of dinosaurs... The latest genetic clues and fossil finds suggest that at least three lineages of modern birds arose during the Cretaceous period and survived a mass extinction 66 million years ago... These discoveries are helping us better understand how birds evolved and how they're related to each other, from the tiny hummingbird to the towering ostrich.[73]

THE SHRINKAGE

How could giant dinosaurs shrink to tiny birds? As usual with the evolution fantasy, all that is needed is the miracle of time. With time all things are possible:

How Dinosaurs Shrank and Became Birds

Modern birds appeared to emerge in a snap of evolutionary time. But new research illuminates the long series of evolutionary changes that made the transformation possible.

Modern birds descended from a group of two-legged dinosaurs known as theropods, whose members include the towering *Tyrannosaurus rex* and the smaller velociraptors. The theropods most closely related to avians generally weighed between 100 and 500 pounds—giants compared to most modern birds—and they had large snouts, big teeth, and not much between the ears. A velociraptor, for example, had a skull like a coyote's and a brain roughly the size of a pigeon's.

For decades, paleontologists' only fossil link between birds and dinosaurs was archaeopteryx, a hybrid creature with feathered wings but with the teeth and long bony tail of a dinosaur. These animals appeared to have acquired their birdlike features—feathers, wings and flight—in just 10 million years, a mere flash in evolutionary time. "Archaeopteryx seemed to emerge fully fledged with the characteristics of modern birds," said Michael Benton, a paleontologist at the University of Bristol in England.

To explain this miraculous metamorphosis, scientists evoked a theory often referred to as "hopeful monsters." According to this idea, major evolutionary leaps require large-scale genetic changes that are qualitatively different from the routine modifications within a species. Only such substantial alterations on a short timescale, the story went, could account for the sudden transformation from a 300-pound theropod to the sparrow-size prehistoric bird *Iberomesornis*.[74]

When I first heard that evolution believers believed birds were once dinosaurs, I thought they must be joking. They weren't:

Are Birds Really Dinosaurs?

> Ask your average paleontologist who is familiar with the phylogeny of vertebrates and they will probably tell you that yes, birds (avians) are dinosaurs. Using proper terminology, birds are avian dinosaurs; other dinosaurs are non-avian dinosaurs, and (strange as it may sound) birds are technically considered reptiles. Overly technical? Just semantics? Perhaps, but still good science.[75]

This is not "good science." And those who think it is must think that science is synonymous with the human imagination, which knows no boundaries.

We have been looking at this massive animal in the light of scientific discoveries that are more than the imaginations of men. We have the complete skeletons of dinosaurs, something that Bible commentators of past centuries lacked:

> The main features of the dinosaurs are unknown, apart from the size of their bones, which indicates that some of them were much larger than any known land animal alive today. Consequently, because of our ignorance here, there is nothing in the passage to eliminate this possibility!

> It is not surprising that before fossils of large extinct animals were found in great numbers, older conservative commentators only tried to identify Behemoth with some of the largest known living animals (even though none of these animals are suitable). The possibility of very large extinct animals did not really occur to them!

The whole passage in Job 40 concerning Behemoth certainly suggests a large animal, and no known living animal fits the passage adequately (for various reasons, including the detailed habitat presented).

The most natural interpretation of the key clause Job 40:17a is that the tail of Behemoth is compared to a cedar for its great size, and there is nothing in the context which contradicts this possibility, even though the exact sense of the verb is extremely difficult to determine.

Consequently, the most reasonable interpretation (which also takes the whole passage into account) is that Behemoth was a large animal, now extinct, which had a large tail. Thus some type of extinct dinosaur should still be considered a perfectly reasonable possibility according to our present state of knowledge.[76]

FISHING WITH SAM

I could see a man ahead of me, in his late fifties or early sixties, walking with a small dog. He was rather tall and heavyset, was wearing a sun hat, and had his nose plastered with sunscreen. I said, "Nice dog; what's his name?" He replied that it was Coco. I told him that it was appropriate because the dog was a cocoa color. Then I handed him a Ten Commandments coin.

As he took it he said that I'd already given him one, and that I was "religious." I told him I wasn't religious and religion does nothing but cause trouble. As he walked away he began asking me questions, which was rather strange. I followed him and found out that he walked because he had to exercise, owing to the fact that he was a diabetic.

The man's name was Tom, and he began to give me almost every argument in the book against the things of God. Why does God let people suffer? Religion causes wars. I explained that more than 90 percent of wars were secular—like the First and Second World Wars and the Korean and Vietnam Wars. He said that he believed in science, and not in religion—which required a blind faith. I told him that nobody has *faith* that there was a builder that built a building. The building *proves* there was a builder, and faith isn't required.

The same with the case of a painting and a painter, and creation and the Creator. We know that God exists because of what we see around us, and that when the Bible speaks of faith it's talking of a *trust* that we have in God. Then I gave some examples of how we trust pilots and doctors. He had so many arguments that I asked him if he ate fish. When he said he did, I told him to handle these questions in the same way he ate fish. Put the bones aside.

We went through the Ten Commandments, talked about Judgment Day, the existence of Hell, and the fact that he was going there. When Tom said he wasn't concerned about Hell because he didn't believe in it, I said that he may not be concerned, but I was. I was horrified at the thought of him receiving justice from the hand of God and ending up there. He said, "You don't even know me."

"I know that your name is Tom, that you're a diabetic, that you're a lying, thieving, blasphemous adulterer at heart, that you like dogs, and that you have the integrity to pick up a deposit your dog leaves" (which he did).

He smiled, and then I shared the gospel with him, and handed him a gift card. Tom seemed quite touched, and as he walked away, he said, "Thank you for the inspiring words," which I found very encouraging.

USING SCIENCE IN THE BIBLE

Here are portions of a number of witnessing encounters (transcribed from one of our videos) using scientific facts in the Bible.

Ray: "Oscar, do you believe the Bible?"

Oscar: "Yes, but I don't think you should take it in a very literal sense."

Ray: "Can you be specific? You mean Jesus didn't literally rise from the dead, or God didn't literally create the earth in six days? What do you mean?"

Oscar: "No, I don't believe Jesus rose from the dead."

Ray: "Juan, do you believe the Bible?"

Juan: "Not particularly. No."

Ray: "Do you think there are mistakes in the Bible?"

Juan: "I do think there are mistakes in the Bible."

Ray: "Can you think of any?"

Juan: "Well, it's written over 3,500 years ago. So, a lot of translation issues might have occurred."

Ray: "Do you think that God could have preserved His Word? If you pass a note to someone, it might change as they pass on the message. But if the person goes *with* the message and preserves it, it is not going to change. And God has preserved His Word. Juan, I've been reading the Bible every day without fail for nearly 44 years, and I have found no mistakes in the Bible. I found *seeming* contradictions, but the mistakes have been *my* mistakes—I just haven't understood something. The Bible is supernatural in origin. Do you know it contains scientific facts written thousands of years before men discover them? Did you know that?"

Juan: "I did not. What scientific facts would these be?"

Ray: "The book of Isaiah says that the earth hangs upon nothing, Job speaks of the earth's free float in space. The book of Leviticus says the life of the flesh is in the blood. If you go and see a doctor and you give him your blood, he can tell how your flesh is doing because it contains information. We didn't discover *that* until recent years. They used to blood-let people a hundred and fifty years ago, thinking that would do them good. Now we put blood *into* people because we know the life of your flesh is in your blood . . . So if you face God on Judgment Day and He judges you by the Ten Commandments—we've looked at four of them—are you going to be innocent or guilty?"

Oscar: "I'd be pretty guilty."

Ray: "Would you go to Heaven or Hell?"

Oscar: "I don't know. It's up to God to decide."

Ray: "He has already told us: All liars will have their part on the lake of fire. No thief, no blasphemer, no adulterer will inherit the kingdom of God. So what are you going to do on Judgment Day? How are you going to justify yourself? Do you think I'm telling the truth or do you think I'm lying?"

Oscar: "You know, you believe in what you believe in. I choose not to believe."

Ray: "So what part don't you believe that I've spoken about? Your beliefs matter. If you are walking along a path and you *believe* the path is safe, you'll just keep going. But if you *believe* there is a landmine right in front of you, you'll go around it. So your beliefs control your actions. If you believe that God is like a dumb idol that doesn't care about justice or truth, you're going to stay in your sins, and you'll end up in Hell. This is *so* serious. So, believe God's Word. He speaks the truth; He doesn't lie. How old are you?"

Oscar: "19."

Ray: "I don't believe that. How old are you?"

Oscar: "19."

Ray: "Nah, I don't believe that. Where do you live? What city?"

Oscar: "Huh?"

Ray: "I don't believe that either. Isn't that an insult to you—if I don't have faith in you?"

Oscar: "Yeah."

Ray: "If you are a mere man and you are insulted by my lack of faith in your word, how much more do you think you insult God by your lack of faith in His Word? You're calling God a liar when you say you don't believe in what He says in His Word, and the Bible says, 'Let none of you depart from the living God through an *evil* heart of unbelief.' You can never establish a relationship with any human being without trust. Saying, 'I like you as a girl-friend but I don't trust you,' is not going to last. Say to your brain surgeon, 'I don't trust you,' or your doctor, or your dentist, 'I don't trust you,' or your banker, 'I don't trust you,' or your pilot. No, you put faith in these people even though they can let you down. How much more should you trust the God who cannot lie? So, think about the sin of unbelief, 'I don't believe what God says,' because you can establish the Bible as inspired—it is God's word, man. I wouldn't lie to you, and I've told you the gospel truth today. I want you to at least think about that . . . would you do that?"

Oscar: "Yeah, I will."

* * *

Ray: "Angel, do you ever think about your own death?"

Angel: "Yeah."

Ray: "Are you afraid of dying?"

Angel: "Yes, I am."

Ray: "You can do something about it. Did you know that?"

Angel: "What can I do about it?"

Ray: "God can grant you everlasting life. If you are in an elevator on the 85th floor and you have no faith in the cables, you are going to be terrified. Isn't that right?"

Angel: "Yes."

Ray: "If someone takes you down and says, 'Look at these cables, they are four inches thick, there's ten of them. There is no way that they can break,' your knowledge will give you faith that will release you of fear. And God can give you knowledge that will explode your faith and take away the fear. Do you think you are a good person? Are you going to Heaven when you die?"

Angel: "I hope. I mean, God gives forgiveness, right?"

Ray: "Have you lied and stolen?"

Angel: "Yes, I have."

Ray: "You are a lying thief? Have you ever used God's name in vain?"

Angel: "I don't know. I think maybe once."

Ray: "It's called blasphemy. And even if you do it once—in

the Old Testament, death sentence. It is *that* serious. You know what God did so you don't have to go to Hell? He did something incredible."

Angel: "What did He do?"

Ray: "He became a human being 2,000 years ago and suffered and died on the cross to take the punishment for the sin of the world. You and I broke God's Law and Jesus paid our fine. If you are in court, even though you are guilty, if someone pays your fine, the judge can let you go. God can let you go—He can forgive your case, your sins—in an instant and grant you the gift of everlasting life because He is rich in mercy. And if you repent and trust in Jesus who died on a cross and rose again on the third day, God will forgive every secret sin you've ever committed and grant you the gift of everlasting life. Let me tell you about the integrity of God... do you think He can do everything?"

Angel: "Yes, He is God."

Ray: "The Bible says there is something God cannot do. It is *impossible* for God to lie. And the Bible uses the word 'impossible' because lying and deceitfulness are repulsive, are so disgusting to God, He would never do it. That means you can trust His integrity; you can trust His promises. That means when God says it in the Bible, you can trust it. Did you know that the Bible is full of scientific and medical facts, written thousands of years before man discovered them?"

Angel: "Really?"

Ray: "It speaks of the earth's free float in space, Isaiah 40: 'The earth hangs upon nothing.' Speaks of the earth being round: 'He who sits upon the circle of the earth.' Speaks of quarantining: lepers had to dwell alone. We didn't understand quarantine until recent years...If people would have understood this, literally millions of lives would have been saved through the years, because we wouldn't have spread diseases."

Angel: "If people would have read the Bible and believed it, they would have known, right?"

Ray: "Read the Bible and believed it; yes, they would have known, and lives would have been saved. Do you think I'm telling the truth about how God can grant you everlasting life in an instant?"

Angel: "Yes."

Ray: "You have to do two things to be saved—repent and trust Christ. When are you doing to do that?"

Angel: "As soon as possible."

Ray: "Today?"

Angel: "I think I can do it today...yes."

Ray: "It's just a matter of apologizing to God for your sins and saying, 'Lord I trust you, You cannot lie, I trust Your integrity. I'm going to lean myself upon You and trust You with my eternal salvation.' Does it make sense?"

Angel: "Yes."

Ray: "Can I pray with you?"

Angel: "Yes."

* * *

Ray: "It wouldn't make any difference to you to know the Bible is full of medical and scientific facts?"

Rod: "Not really."

Ray: "You know, if you are on a plane that's about to crash and you didn't see your need of putting on a parachute, one of the best things I could do for you would be to hang you out of the plane by your ankles for five seconds. And when you come back in the plane, your good sense would kick in and you'd say, 'Give me that parachute!' because you know you are in danger. Knowing the Bible is full of medical and scientific facts won't bring you to Christ, but knowing you are in danger will. Do you think you are in danger when you die?"

Rod: "You are in danger in everyday life, I mean . . . "

Ray: "I mean *eternal* danger. I don't mean the danger of being hit by a car, I mean in danger of ending up in Hell. Let me hang you out of the plane by your ankles just for a second. It won't take long, and it won't be very pleasant but it will be very profitable for you. How many lies have you told in your whole life?"

Rod: "Oh, thousands, I'm sure."

Ray: "Have you stolen something?"

Rod: "I'm sure plenty of times when I was a kid, I've stolen. I mean, kids see something shiny they like, they grab it."

Ray: "Gold or diamonds. Have you ever used God's name in vain?"

Rod: "Oh, yeah."

Ray: "Jesus said, 'If you look at a woman to lust for her, you've committed adultery with her in your heart.' Have you ever done that?"

Rod: "Yes."

Ray: "So, Rod, you have just told me you are lying, thieving, blasphemous adulterer at heart, and you have to face God on Judgment Day. When you stand before Him and He judges you by the Commandments, are you are going to be innocent or guilty?"

Rod: "Guilty."

Ray: "Heaven or Hell?"

Rod: "Hell."

Ray: "This is where your good sense should kick in, when you say, 'Hey, I need a Savior, I need to put on the Lord Jesus Christ . . . I need my sins forgiven, and God has provided a Savior, one who died on a cross for our sins, took our punishment so we wouldn't have to go to Hell.' If you are in court, even though you are guilty, if someone pays your fine, the judge can let you go. And God can let you go; He can let you live forever because of what Jesus did through His death and resurrection. What you have to do is repent and trust in Him, like you trust a parachute. 'Put on the Lord Jesus Christ,' the Scriptures say. So would you at least think of this, Rod?"

Rod: "I'll give it a thought."

Ray: "You have a little kid you love?"

Rod: "Two of them."

Ray: "What are you going to say to them when they say, 'Daddy, why am I gonna die?'"

Rod: "Well, my daughter is currently growing up a Christian. She's ten years old."

Ray: "You're talking to me today because of her prayers."

QUESTIONS TO CONSIDER

1. What are four characteristics of the creature described in Job 40:15–24?

2. Why could this creature not be an elephant or hippopotamus, as some believe?

3. What does the word "behemoth" mean?

4. What does the world think happened to dinosaurs?

5. See Genesis 1:24,25. When was the dinosaur created?

6. If Job was able to "behold" a dinosaur, what does that tell us about whether they lived with humans?

7. What do these passages in Job do to your faith in the Bible?

11

AIR POLLUTION
AND SCIENCE

Sam and I were at the skateboard park. It was a great place to share the gospel and to get interviews for our YouTube channel and TV program. This particular day was extremely hot, and I heard one of the skateboarders say that he was going home because he was thirsty. That's when I had an idea. I raced home on my bike, grabbed seven bottles of water, and excitedly raced back to the park.

But by the time I got back, they had moved away from the heat and were sitting under the shadow of a large tree. It was a bit of an anticlimax as I gave them the water, because they had moved to the cooler area. But two of the seven sounded grateful.

The next day I showed up at the park, and as I sat on my bike watching them skateboard, I noticed that a skateboarder (about fifty yards from me) waved enthusiastically. His wave made me feel that my rushing back home in the heat was well worth it. He didn't look familiar, so I surmised that word got around about my kind deed.

A minute or so later I noticed two of them were now enthusiastically waving at me. Word sure got around. Good works speak volumes. Then it dawned on me: I was standing by the landing side of a ramp, and they were telling me to get out of the way.

Our agenda as Christians is to tell sinners to get out of the way. They must flee from God's wrath or they will perish. However, telling sinners to get out of the way of His anger doesn't always come with a direct warning.

A young pastor went to a small town in Texas, where he kept getting himself in hot water. He's one of the most zealous Christians I know. He would rather die than compromise the gospel. But he had a problem. He was annoying almost the whole town. He was even upsetting his church elders as well as the rest of his congregation, because he kept preaching the gospel everywhere he went.

So he asked me if he should compromise by slowing down. I said that he should say to his elders, "This is what I'm going to say after every service: 'If you would like to talk further about your eternal salvation, I would love to speak with you.'" I told him to tell them that was all he would say. Then I added, "If I were you, I would deliver groceries to every home in your town. Tell your elders that's what you want to do, because you want your church to be known as a church that is rich in good works. And when you deliver the groceries to each house, leave them at the doorstep. You're not trying to get a foot in the door. Leave a simple letter (without your letterhead), just stating your name, that you're from the local church and you're here to help them in any way you can. Say that they can call on you for *anything* practical—mowing lawns, painting walls, fixing fences, or trimming a hedge. Don't even say 'God bless' at the end. The Bible says that by your well doing you will put to silence the ignorance of foolish men. Living in a small town is very similar to living with your family. You *cannot* preach to them incessantly. You have to show them your faith by your works, and the same applies in a small town."

This is simply the exercise of discretion. You don't have to hit the ball out of the park to win a game. You can sometimes bunt.

LA AIR POLLUTION

Our ministry is located in Los Angeles County, about fifteen minutes north of Disneyland. When we first came to the US back in the late 1980s, the air pollution was horrific. There were days when you could actually see the invisible air currents in the sky because the pollution was so thick, it exposed it. Over the years it has thankfully improved. However, one thing I've noticed as I pass through airports in that postcards showing Los Angeles have obviously been taken after a storm when the air is super fresh and clean.

Most of us think that when the air is clean after the storm, the rain has washed away the pollution. However, it's far more complex than that. God has set in motion something amazing that happens to the air molecules. The air we breathe consists of O_2 (oxygen). When there is an electrical charge—a lightning strike—the molecules combine to form O_3 (ozone). In the process, the O_3 attaches itself to the pollution and disintegrates it on a molecular level.

The lightning of the wrath of God has a similar effect spiritually. Through the fear of the Lord men depart from the pollution of evil—at a molecular level. When we truly fear God, we don't try to hide secret sins (because we know there's no such thing). The gospel has the power not just to cleanse us of sin, but to completely annihilate it. The grace of God in Christ removes our transgressions as far as the east is from the west. That's an incalculable distance. So never fear preaching the fear of God. Never be afraid to make the sinner afraid. You do him a great favor.

HUMANS AND CANINES

It's not good to compare human beings to common dogs. This is because it's an insult to dogs. But I will do it anyway.

If you're a *real* dog lover, you perhaps do something I do. If I see Sam lying down on the floor, I lie down with him, go eye-to-eye and talk to him. I feed key words into the conversation. I say things like, "We went on the BIKE today. We didn't see any CATS or SQUIRRELS. We saw a DOG, though..." Each key word feeds thoughts into his eyes. You can see the processing taking place. Without fail, the second he sees me heading toward the lowly floor, his tail wags big time. The personal closeness thrills him.

Doesn't it thrill you when you think of the incarnation? God came way down to our level. In Christ, we get to see Him eye-to-eye, up close and personal. Like the disciples, our hearts burn within us as we see Him face-to-face in the Scriptures. The Bible contains the words that set our minds processing information about how amazing God is. But Scripture climaxes in the love expressed in the cross, leaving us in wide-eyed awe:

> But we see Jesus, who was made a little lower than the angels, for the suffering of death crowned with glory and honor, that He, by the grace of God, might taste death for everyone. (Hebrews 2:9)

FISHING WITH SAM

I could see a distant figure of someone sitting on a picnic seat. As we approached him, I saw that it was a man in his early twenties. I asked, "Did I give you one of these?" as I handed him a Ten Commandments coin, and asked if he thought there was an afterlife. He was a loner, dressed in black, his head was shaven, had some sort of sore on his forehead, and he was very soft-spoken.

His appearance and demeanor made me a little nervous. I changed the subject and asked if he had a dog. That caused him to lift his voice slightly as he spoke about his beloved pit bull. I introduced myself, asked for his name and if he would go on camera. Danny was adamant that he didn't want to go on camera. When I asked if I could speak to him off camera, he said he didn't want to speak any further. I took a risk and just said, "Let me ask you a couple of questions," and took him through the Commandments anyway.

After we had finished talking about the necessity of repentance and faith in Jesus, I said, "Danny, I want to thank you for listening to me when you didn't want to." When I gave him a Subway gift card, he said, "I'm sorry I was so stubborn. Some people try to change your beliefs." Apparently, he didn't see that as my agenda. It was encouraging to hear him say that.

As Sam and I rode away, I was pleased that I too was stubborn. I hope that your love for this lost world is also stubborn.

12

SCIENCE AND THE PROBLEM OF EVIL

Well-known atheist Sam Harris once said, "Either God can do nothing to stop catastrophes . . . or he doesn't care to, or he doesn't exist. God is either impotent, evil, or imaginary. Take your pick, and choose wisely."

Perhaps this eloquent atheist isn't being deliberately manipulative in this celebrated answer to the issue of suffering. However, it is intellectually unfair to speak of a problem and limit the answer. All he gives is an artificial either/or.

Mr. Harris imagines an impotent Creator—one who has created the complexity of DNA and the intricacies of the entire universe, yet has become useless for some unknown reason. Or He can help humanity, but He is evil by not stepping up to the moral plate. But this argument can't be used by Harris, because he is an atheist. For him there is no objective and unchanging standard for morality. How could there be? For him, life is simply what society accepts at a particular time in history. There is no ultimate evil or good because he has nothing by which to judge good or evil. So to accuse God of being evil is disingenuous.

The third choice is that God is imaginary. This is the choice Harris has embraced. But that would be to crown yourself a fool—because you are choosing the scientific impossibility that nothing created everything. It's not a choice for any rational creature. It's cerebral lunacy. We must therefore be open to one or more other explanations.

If a psychopath rapes and kills a dozen young girls, what moral *obligation* does the judge in his case have toward him? Is he obliged to ensure the man is happy as he sits in his cell for justice to take place? Of course not. He should have the minimum of comforts as he awaits execution. The judge's only moral obligation is to see that justice is done.

The criminal may come to the conclusion that the judge can do nothing to help him, that he doesn't care, or that the judge doesn't exist. But those judgments are made by him in ignorance of the judge's love of justice. They demean the judge's character by assuming he is morally obligated to help the criminal when he's not. All he owes him is justice for his heinous crimes.

Unregenerate humanity ignorantly exalts the character of man and tears down the character of God. As an atheist, Sam Harris makes the assumption that God is morally obligated to play housemaid to all of humanity. This is the fruit of idolatry. He refuses the light of Scripture and in his darkness creates his own image of God, when the Bible reveals our Creator as the very source of Justice:

Righteousness and justice are the foundation of Your throne; mercy and truth go before Your face. (Psalm 89:14)

He is the Judge of the Universe, and we are desperately wicked criminals waiting to be executed for our crimes. The Bible reveals that He is a fire of burning holiness—so wrath-filled at evil humanity, He gave the entire human race the death sentence. We die because we have sinned against God. Death is the final evidence that He is deadly serious about sin. He has no obligation to ensure our happiness. All He owes us is Justice, and that will be perfectly done on the Day of Judgment.

But look at what happened! The Judge took off His robe and took the place of the criminal so that he could go free.

I am fortunate enough to be friends with a number of high-profile atheists. Unfortunately, Sam Harris is not one of them. But from what I have seen of him on video, he seems to be a reasonable and likable man. We should love all atheists, and extend a merciful attitude toward them because we are aware that they are just where we have once been. Sam Harris can only make judgments with the knowledge he has. The Scriptures tell us that his understanding (and the understanding of every other lost human being) is darkened, and that he is alienated from the life of God through the ignorance that is in him because of the blindness of his heart (see Ephesians 4:18). This, however, is a willful ignorance. He has access to the light, but the Bible tells us that he loves the darkness rather than light, and he will not come to the light because his sinful deeds will be exposed. When the apostle Paul spoke to the Athenians, he spoke of their ignorance and said that God in His great mercy overlooked it, but now He commands all men everywhere to repent (see Acts 17:30). And that is our desperate message to the Sam Harrises of this world. We love them enough to warn them that on Judgment Day, ignorance is not a bush that we can hide behind.

THE PURSUIT OF HAPPINESS

The problem is that we are products of an entitlement mentality. We believe that God is morally obligated to make sure we are happy. This is confirmed in the second paragraph of the United States Declaration of Independence, which starts as follows:

> We hold these truths to be self-evident, that all men are created equal, that they are endowed by their Creator with certain unalienable Rights, that among these are Life, Liberty and the Pursuit of Happiness.

And if we side with the criminal and believe he has the right to be happy, by default the judge becomes evil. A secular source, Stanford Encyclopedia of Philosophy, weighs in on what constitutes "evil":

> Since World War II, moral, political, and legal philosophers have become increasingly interested in the concept of evil. This interest has been partly motivated by ascriptions of "evil" by laymen, social scientists, journalists, and politicians as they try to understand and respond to various atrocities and horrors, such as genocides, terrorist attacks, mass murders, and tortures and killing sprees by psychopathic serial killers. It seems that we cannot capture the moral significance of these actions and their perpetrators by calling them "wrong" or

"bad" or even "very very wrong" or "very very bad." We need the concept of evil.

To avoid confusion, it is important to note that there are at least two concepts of evil: a broad concept and a narrow concept. The broad concept picks out any bad state of affairs, wrongful action, or character flaw. The suffering of a toothache is evil in the broad sense as is a white lie. Evil in the broad sense has been divided into two categories: natural evil and moral evil. Natural evils are bad states of affairs which do not result from the intentions or negligence of moral agents. Hurricanes and toothaches are examples of natural evils. By contrast, moral evils do result from the intentions or negligence of moral agents. Murder and lying are examples of moral evils.

Evil in the broad sense, which includes all natural and moral evils, tends to be the sort of evil referenced in theological contexts, such as in discussions of the problem of evil. The problem of evil is the problem of accounting for evil in a world created by an all-powerful, all-knowing, all-good God. It seems that if the creator has these attributes, there would be no evil in the world. But there is evil in the world. Thus, there is reason to believe that an all-powerful, all-knowing, all-good creator does not exist.[77]

An interesting question to ask unbelievers is, "What do you think God requires of you?"

Most think He requires you to be a morally good person. But the requirement is much greater than that. He *commands* you to love Him with all of your heart, mind, soul, and strength. And it goes even deeper. Jesus said that your love for God should be so great that your love for your husband or wife, brother or sister, or even your own life should seem like hatred compared to the love you have for God.

Here then is the follow-up question for you if you're an unbeliever: "Do you think God has the right to *command* that of you?"

If you say He doesn't, let me ask you, who gave you your eyes? Some might be quick to reply that their parents gave them their eyes. But I guarantee the last thing on your parents' minds when you were conceived was the making of your eyes. If any eyes were being made, it was at each other. Besides, if you became blind and went back to your parents and asked them to make you some more eyes, they would rightly have you examined by a psychiatrist.

13

THE TOP TEN EXCUSES

You may have noticed in reading the witnessing sessions that when the light of God's moral Law exposes a sinner's guilt, he will usually try to justify himself. The feeling of guilt isn't pleasant, and so he attempts to shake it off by offering excuses.

Think of a child who is stealing cookies from the cookie jar in the darkness of night. When his dad turns on the light, he sees that the boy's mouth is covered with chocolate, the lid is off the jar, and cookies are gone. The child is exposed and has two avenues: he will either admit his guilt, or he will attempt to justify himself.

We are *all* guilty of sinning against God (see Romans 3:23). We've been caught with our hand in the cookie jar, chocolate all over our sinful face, and we therefore have two avenues. We can either try to cover our sins, or we can confess them. But here is the warning:

He who covers his sins will not prosper, but whoever confesses and forsakes them will have mercy. (Proverbs 28:13)

It is a strong consolation to us as believers who want to reach the unsaved, knowing that the light of God's Law awakens the sinner's inner light—his dormant conscience:

They show that the essential requirements of the Law are written in their hearts; and their conscience [their sense of right and wrong, their moral choices] bearing witness and their thoughts alternately accusing or perhaps defending them. (Romans 2:15, AMP)

In other words, the conscience bears *witness* to the Law. It is a witness for the prosecution, and it will fight for the case of his guilt.

After the apostle Paul explains this relationship of the Law and the human conscience, he shows how to use the Law to bring the knowledge of sin:

You who preach that a man should not steal, do you steal? You who say, "Do not commit adultery," do you commit adultery? (Romans 2:21,22)

You've just asked a sinner similar questions and he's admitted that he's a liar, a thief, a blasphemer, and an adulterer at heart. The light is on. His hand is clearly in the cookie jar. His conscience therefore begins to do its duty, and as it accuses him he will predictably try to justify himself.

Here are some simple responses to excuses that guilty sinners use to try to justify themselves (I hope that they are helpful):

1. "They were just *small* lies—white lies. Nothing serious."
    Sin is so serious to God, it demands the death sentence.
    The Bible says, "Lying lips are an abomination to the Lord"
    (Proverbs 12:22).

2. "*Everyone* lies."
    We won't be giving an account for everyone on Judgment
    Day—everyone will give an account of himself to God. If
    you are stopped for speeding on the freeway by a police of-
    ficer, it won't do any good to say that *everybody* speeds. The
    Law will hold you *personally* accountable for your crimes.
    What others do is irrelevant to your case.

3. "That was in the past."
    Everything is in the past. Even this sentence is in the past.
    Telling a judge that you robbed the bank but that was "in
    the past," thinking that he will let you go because it was in
    the past, is ridiculous.

4. "I do good things."
    A criminal may tell a judge that he does good deeds, but they
    are irrelevant to his case. Criminal law judges only accord-
    ing to the crime, not your good deeds. God will judge you
    according to your crimes, and the crimes only.

5. "My God is loving and kind."
    It's called "idolatry" when we make up a god to suit our-
    selves. The God you have to face is loving and kind, but He
    is also just and holy, and will by no means clear the guilty
    (see Exodus 34:7).

6. "I don't believe in God."

That doesn't matter. You still have to face Him on Judgment Day whether you believe in Him or not.

7. "God committed genocide when He drowned millions in the flood."

You are a self-admitted lying thief, a blasphemer, and an adulterer at heart. You are in no place to accuse the Judge of being evil.

8. "I don't believe in the Ten Commandments."

Ignorance of the Law is no excuse. God wrote the Commandments on your heart via your conscience. On Judgment Day you will be without excuse.

9. "I don't care if I go to Hell."

Two seconds in Hell will change your mind about that, and there will be no way out.

10. "I don't believe in Hell."

If a criminal has been condemned to death and says he doesn't believe in the death sentence, his unbelief doesn't change reality. God *will* have His Day of Justice.

Always keep in mind that you're not out to win an argument. You simply want him to see that he is in horrific danger, so that he will seek the safety of the Savior. What you are hoping to do is dash his false hope. You are putting him up the river Niagara without a paddle. This is in the hope that he will reach out to the only rope being thrown from the shore. The Law is the way to help him see that taking hold of the rope is a rational step of self-preservation. It makes the good news of the gospel make sense. It prepares the way for grace. I will never forget having my own hope dashed on the night of my conversion many years ago. I looked at the words of Jesus and found comfort in them. He said,

> "You have heard that it was said to those of old, 'You shall not commit adultery.'" (Matthew 5:27)

That is a wonderful verse in the Sermon on the Mount. It told me that I would make it to Heaven, because I had kept that Commandment. It gave me comfort and hope of salvation. But then in the next verse I read the word "But" and it destroyed my hope in a second:

> "But I say to you that whoever looks at a woman to lust for her has already committed adultery with her in his heart." (Matthew 5:28)

His words put an arrow of death in my sinful chest. All hope was gone. I was undone, without hope, heading for Hell. It was then that I cried in my heart, "What must I do to be made *right?*" For the first time in my blind, sinful, and unregenerate state, I began to thirst for righteousness, and that prepared me for the good news of the gospel.

ONE LAST POINT

I'm so grateful that you have taken the time to read this book. If you're an unbeliever, please think about your eternal salvation. Again, I don't necessarily want to convince you that the Bible is the Word of God at this moment. I first want to convince you that you are in great danger, and that you desperately need the Savior.

If you're a believer, please share your faith. Pick up the moral Law and use it as Jesus did. I want to especially bring to your remembrance something stated earlier in the book, because it is so important.

Do you remember the time those young men came around to my home to deliver the gazebo? And do you remember how I was the chief of chickens, because I didn't have a plan? I hadn't prepared in my mind to share the gospel with them. This is such an essential truth. Almost every time I have chickened out, it was because there was a lack of mental preparation. I hadn't determined to overcome the fear that I knew I would get the moment I approached a sinner to share the gospel. The apostle Paul, however, had a plan. Look at his words:

> For I *determined* not to know anything among you except Jesus Christ and Him crucified. I was with you in weakness, in fear, and in much trembling. And my speech and my preaching were not with persuasive words of human wisdom, but in demonstration of the Spirit and of power... (1 Corinthians 2:2–4, emphasis added)

Paul had fear, but he "determined." He was prepared in his mind to overcome fear. And if you do the same by taking the time to plan out what you are going to say, how you are not going to let fear get the victory, you will overcome it and share the gospel with an unsaved person... and there is nothing more important than that. As I've said many times over the years, you will approach the person dragging your feet, and come back clicking your heels.

Allow me to leave you with the wonderfully wise words of my favorite preacher, Charles Spurgeon:

> Open up the spirituality of the Law as our Lord did, and show how it is broken by evil thoughts, intents, and imaginations. By this means many sinners will be pricked in their hearts. Old Robbie Flockhart used to say, "It is of no use trying to sew with the silken thread of the gospel unless we pierce a way for it with the sharp needle of the Law." The Law goes first, like the needle, and draws the gospel thread after it: therefore preach concerning sin, righteousness, and judgment to come. Let such language as that of the fifty-first Psalm be often explained: show that God requires truth in the inward parts, and that purging with sacrificial blood is absolutely needful. Aim at the heart. Probe the wound and touch the very quick of the soul. Spare not the sterner themes, for men must be wounded before they can be healed, and slain before they can be made alive. No man will ever put on the robe of Christ's righteousness till he is stripped of his fig leaves, nor will he wash in the fount of mercy till he perceives his filthiness. Therefore, my brethren, we must not cease to declare the Law, its demands, its threatenings, and the sinner's multiplied breaches of it.[78]

May God bless you and your labors for Him.

NOTES

1. Christopher Hitchens vs. Douglas Wilson debate: "Is Christianity Good for the World?" October 29, 2008, The King's College, tinyurl.com/y75xa6w5.
2. "51% of Churchgoers Don't Know of the Great Commission," Barna Group, March 27, 2018, tinyurl.com/y9jlwkq2.
3. Bill Bright, *The Coming Revival* (Orlando, FL: NewLife Publications, 1995), p. 65.
4. "Astronomy—Earth Hangs In Space," StreetWitnessing.org, tinyurl.com/jb3fdbf.
5. "Is the Bible Scientifically Accurate?" Alpha Omega Institute, tinyurl.com/ybk8xrcj.
6. 500 Questions about God & Christianity, May 21, 2011, tinyurl.com/y96oqlrg.
7. Ibid.
8. 1 Samuel 2:8 Commentary, *John Gill's Exposition of the Bible*, tinyurl.com/yalkh3qx.
9. Eric McLamb, "How Much Does Earth Weigh?" Ecology.com, September 8, 2008, tinyurl.com/yb2jy54n.
10. "Are we really all made of stardust?" Physics.org, physics.org/article-questions.asp?id=52.
11. Elizabeth Howell, "Humans Really Are Made of Stardust, and a New Study Proves It," Space.com, January 10, 2017, tinyurl.com/ya7awnzt.
12. Antony Flew, Wikipedia.com, wikipedia.org/wiki/Antony_Flew.
13. Antony Flew, *There Is a God: How the World's Most Notorious Atheist Changed His Mind* (New York: HarperCollins, 2007), p. 75.
14. Ibid., pp. 88–89.
15. "Cotton and U.S. Currency," Cotton.org, tinyurl.com/y8sms4ng.
16. "U.S. Currency: How Money is Made—Paper and Ink," US Department of the Treasury, Bureau of Engraving and Printing, tinyurl.com/ybxjs5s6.
17. Ibid.
18. Parija Kavilanz, "Guess what? Dollar bills are made of cotton," CNN Money, March 8, 2011, tinyurl.com/ya5acajv.
19. Stuart Wavell, "In the beginning there was something," *The Sunday Times* (UK), December 19, 2004.
20. These are available through LivingWaters.com.

21. Doyle Rice, "Far out: Astronomers discover most distant star ever seen," *USA Today*, April 2, 2018.

22. "How Great Thou Art," © 1949 and 1953 by the Stuart Hine Trust.

23. "What is the biggest star we know?" StarChild, NASA/GSFC, tinyurl.com/y95ufgca.

24. Corey S. Powell, "The Man Who Made Stars and Planets," *Discover* magazine, January 12, 2009.

25. Richard Gray, "Is your dog happy to see you? Look at its eyebrows to find out," *The Telegraph* (UK), July 30, 2013.

26. "The Criminal Justice System: Statistics," rainn.org/statistics/criminal-justice-system.

27. Cathal O'Connell, "What Is Light?" *Cosmos* magazine, June 14, 2016.

28. Colin Barras, "What Is a Ray of Light Made Of?" BBC.com, July 31, 2015.

29. Wayne Jackson, "What Was that 'Light' before the Sun (Genesis 1:3)?" ChristianCourier.com, tinyurl.com/y75xtqzc.

30. Clara Moskowitz, "What Makes Earth Special Compared to Other Planets," SPACE.com, July 8, 2008.

31. World Health Organization, September 12, 2018, who.int/news-room/fact-sheets/detail/cancer.

32. Jennie Cohen, "A Brief History of Bloodletting," *History*, May 30, 2012, tinyurl.com/lmohl49.

33. Lecia Bushak, "Scientists Create Artificial Blood That Can Be Produced On An Industrial Scale: A Limitless Supply Of Blood?" *Medical Daily*, April 15, 2014, tinyurl.com/yb5cugbc.

34. Sophie Weiner, "How Quickly Can We Circumnavigate the World?" *Popular Mechanics*, March 31, 2018.

35. Melissa Hogenboom, "We have known that Earth is round for over 2,000 years," BBC.com, January 26, 2016, tinyurl.com/hyzhfrm.

36. Kay Brigham, *Christopher Columbus: His life and discovery in the light of his prophecies* (Terrassa, Barcelona: CLIE Publishers, 1990).

37. As quoted by Paul G. Humber in "Columbus and His Creator," ICR, October 1, 1991, icr.org/article/columbus-his-creator.

38. Flat Earth Society, wiki.tfes.org/Frequently_Asked_Questions.

39. Hogenboom, "We have known that Earth is round for over 2,000 years," BBC.com.

40. Meghan Bartels, "Scientists Used a Super Powerful Cannon to Show How Asteroids Can Carry Water Between Worlds," *Newsweek*, April 25, 2018.

41. Lenntech, Water Chemistry FAQ, tinyurl.com/y963rwum.

42. Bartels, "Scientists Used a Super Powerful Cannon," *Newsweek*.

43. Ibid.

44. Ibid.

45. Effie Munday, "Matthew Fontaine Maury: Pathfinder of the seas," *Creation*, vol. 6, iss. 2, November 1983, pp. 25–28.

46. Rev. T. M. Eddy, "The Sea," *The Ladies' Repository*, vol. 15, iss. 8, August 1855, pp. 460–461.

47. Matt Williams, "What percent of Earth is water?" *Universe Today*, December 2, 2014, tinyurl.com/y99ajxmm.

48. *A Life of Matthew Fontaine Maury*, compiled by Diana Fontaine Maury Corbin (London: Sampson Low, Marston, Searle, & Rivington, Ltd., 1888), pp. 176, 178.

49. Ibid., pp. 158–160.

50. Miriam Kramer, "Let Stephen Hawking blow your mind with what happened before the Big Bang," Mashable.com, March 5, 2018, tinyurl.com/yyn6op9p.

51. Jamie Seidel, "Stephen Hawking says he knows what happened before the dawn of time," News.com.au, March 3, 2018.

52. Ibid.

53. Kramer, "Let Stephen Hawking blow your mind . . . ," Mashable.com.

54. "What Is Weather and Climate?" Mocomi.com, mocomi.com/weather-and-climate.

55. Alecia M. Spooner, "What Is the Hydrologic Cycle?" Dummies.com, tinyurl.com/ydajsftf.

56. Mississippi River Facts, National Park Service, nps.gov/miss/riverfacts.htm.

57. Nola Taylor Redd, "How Old is the Universe?" Space.com, June 7, 2017.

58. Andy Bodle, "How new words are born," *The Guardian*, February 4, 2016, tinyurl.com/yas6q6xr.

59. Tim Lovett, "Thinking Outside the Box," *Answers* magazine, April–June 2007, tinyurl.com/ycgygbqf.

60. Sarah Knapton, "Scientists: Noah's Ark Would Have Floated With 70,000 Animals If Built By Dimensions In The Bible," *The Telegraph*, April 3, 2014.

61. Antony Flew, "How the World's Most Notorious Atheist Changed His Mind," interview with Dr. Benjamin Wiker, October 30, 2007, tinyurl.com/ycp5otw2.

62. Peter Tyson, "A Short History of Quarantine," NOVA, October 11, 2004, tinyurl.com/ycz5tejx.

63. "History of Quarantine," Centers for Disease Control and Prevention, tinyurl.com/y7mcpj39.

64. Philip A. Mackowiak and Paul S. Sehdev, "The Origin of Quarantine," *Clinical Infectious Diseases*, vol. 35, iss. 9, November 1, 2002, pp. 1071–1072, doi.org/10.1086/344062.

65. Matthew Poole, "Commentary on Jude 1:23," *Matthew Poole's English Annotations on the Holy Bible*, studylight.org/commentaries/mpc/jude-1.html.

66. Allan K. Steel, "Could Behemoth have been a dinosaur?" *Journal of Creation*, vol. 15, iss. 2, August 2001, pp. 42–45.

67. *Strong's Concordance*, tinyurl.com/y9fcr98h.

68. Michael Greshko, "Huge Dinosaur Footprints Discovered on Scottish Coast," *National Geographic*, April 2, 2018.

69. Jim Barlow, "A one-two punch may have helped deck the dinosaurs," *Science Daily*, February 7, 2018.

70. Roff Smith, "Here's What Happened the Day the Dinosaurs Died," *National Geographic*, June 11, 2016.

71. "What Killed The Dinosaurs?" University of California Museum of Paleontology, ucmp.berkeley.edu/diapsids/extinction.html.

72. "How Did Dinosaurs Die?" Answers in Genesis, May 1, 2013, tinyurl. com/yaw7phmg.

73. Victoria Jaggard, "These Are the Dinosaurs That Didn't Die," *National Geographic*, May 2018.

74. Emily Singer, "How Dinosaurs Shrank and Became Birds," *Quanta Magazine*, June 12, 2015.

75. "Are Birds Really Dinosaurs?" University of California Museum of Paleontology, ucmp.berkeley.edu/diapsids/avians.html.

76. Allan K. Steel, "Could Behemoth have been a dinosaur?" *Journal of Creation*, vol. 15, iss. 2, August 2001, pp. 42–45.

77. "The Concept of Evil," Stanford Encyclopedia of Philosophy, August 21, 2018, plato.stanford.edu/entries/concept-evil.

78. Charles Spurgeon, "Lecture 23: On Conversion as Our Aim," *Lectures to My Students*.

EVIDENCE BIBLE
Ray Comfort

Apologetic answers to over 200 questions, thousands of comments, and over 130 informative articles will help you better comprehend and share the Christian faith.

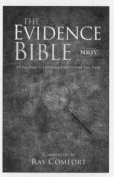

ISBN: 9780882705255

SCIENTIFIC FACTS IN THE BIBLE
Ray Comfort

Most people, even Christians, don't know that the Bible contains a wealth of incredible scientific, medical, and prophetic facts. That being so, the implications are mind boggling.

ISBN: 9780882708799

HOW TO KNOW GOD EXISTS
Ray Comfort

Does God exist, or does He not? In this compelling book, Ray Comfort argues the case with simple logic and common sense. This book will convince you that belief in God is reasonable and rational—a matter of fact and not faith.

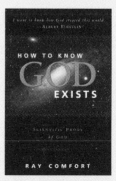

ISBN: 9780882704326

SCHOOL OF BIBLICAL EVANGELISM
Ray Comfort & Kirk Cameron

This comprehensive study offers 101 lessons on thought-provoking topics including basic Christian doctrines, cults and other religions, creation/evolution, and more. Learn how to share your faith simply, effectively, and biblically... the way Jesus did.

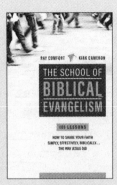

ISBN: 9780882709680

WAY OF THE MASTER STUDENT EDITION
Ray Comfort & Allen Atzbi

Youth today are being inundated with opposing messages, and desperately need to hear the truth of the gospel. How can you reach them? Sharing the good news is much easier than you think ... by using some timeless principles.

ISBN: 9781610364737